Boston
for
Families

A Comprehensive Guide to the City

Information gathered for this book was current at publication, but things change all the time. Places close, change hours or prices, and move.

Printed in the United States of America.

Photos © Kim Foley MacKinnon, unless otherwise noted.
Cover photo © Kim Foley MacKinnon

Booklocker.com, Inc.
2004

Kim Foley MacKinnon
www.kfmwriter.com

Boston for Families

A Comprehensive Guide to the City

By Kim Foley MacKinnon

About the Author

Kim Foley MacKinnon is a long-time Boston resident and mother of a five-year-old daughter. She has written widely about Boston, family life, travel and people for a variety of publications, including *The Boston Globe, Boston Parents' Paper,* and *Parents* magazine among others. This is her second guidebook about Boston.

Author's Note
So many people were involved in making this book happen.
Thank you to all of the people who always support me.
You know who you are and so do I.

Table of Contents

Introduction

I am not a native Bostonian. Loving Boston came slowly to me. I moved here more than 10 years ago with every expectation of moving on again in a few years. But like many people who think Boston will be a temporary home, I was hooked. Now I can't imagine living anywhere else. Boston seems small and large, old and new, all at once. I never tire of exploring the city and it never disappoints.

Leonard P. Zakim Bridge © *Greater Boston Convention & Visitors Bureau*

Boston is rich in history – the word "first" and "old" before an attraction in this guide will become familiar to you soon. But it doesn't remain stuck in the past. It can't. With more than 50 colleges and universities in the area, Boston is constantly changing and growing, adding new firsts all the time. Thousands of students keep the city energized, many of them falling in love with Boston, like I did, and making it their home. At the same time it embraces the new, Boston is fiercely attached to its history. We've saved many sites that played an important role in our history and you'll find them flush against new skyscrapers and office buildings.

As any parent will tell you, having a child makes you look at the world in a different way. I am happy to look at Boston through a different lens. My daughter is lucky to grow up in the city. She takes it for granted that Boston Common and the Public Garden are her personal playgrounds. Her preschool regularly checks books out of the grand Central Boston Public Library (the oldest free public library; the first library with a children's room – see what I mean about "old" and "first"?) in Copley Square. While these seem commonplace to her now, someday she'll know the privilege she had learning in the Hub.

I hope this book conveys the excitement and adventure Boston holds for us and for anyone, especially families, willing to open their eyes to all that is around them.

How This Book Works

Like many metropolitan areas, Boston is a series of little neighborhoods. It is called "America's Walking City" with good reason – it's much easier to walk than drive in any one area. It makes sense then to organize this book by neighborhood, rather than by activities or categories that might send you back and forth across town, wasting precious vacation time and trying your kids' patience. Within each neighborhood, sights are given in alphabetical order. At the end of every section, look for "Take 10," where I've listed the area's best playground for when the kids just need to run around and be loud. An outdoor break, even if lasts just for a few minutes, can buy you time later at a museum or restaurant. Chapter One gives a quick orientation to the city and how to get around. Chapter Two is where you'll find the bulk of local activities. Driving in Boston is an art form not even done successfully by most natives. Whenever practical, I've given directions to sites using public transportation. If you are driving, be prepared to get lost, but don't panic. Boston isn't that big.

One thing Boston has is a surplus of walking trails and tours. Everyone has heard of the Freedom Trail, but what about the Black Heritage Trail? Or the Literary Trail? Chapter Three details the best and most interesting ones of the lot. Whether you go on your own or opt for a guided tour, taking in the city this way is a great orientation. Since going to the theatre or a symphony are more planned events than something you do while sightseeing, I've put them by themselves, in Chapter Four. Almost every higher cultural institution in Boston schedules special family- or child-oriented events. To give a comprehensive listing of hotels and restaurants would be beyond the scope of this book, but I have listed a few that are super family-friendly. Not everyone knows where you can have Sunday brunch in your pajamas or where parents can eat gourmet meals while the kids play within sight in an activity area set up just for them. Chapter Five covers the top picks in the city.

Museums are to be found at every turn in Boston. Higher cultural institutions aren't always the most exciting of visits for many kids, especially little ones (unless it's the Children's Museum, of course). Therefore, where I could, I included details of any programs the museums offer. Some have re-enactments, or crafts days, some have story hours. I think these are great ways to get kids interested and enthusiastic about museums. Many have family activity packs. Be sure to ask. I did not limit the guide to any specific age group. Where appropriate, I've noted whether teenagers or toddlers would be more interested, but hopefully, most sites will interest the whole family.

There are many sights within an easy drive or train ride from Boston, which you'll find in Chapter Six. Even those with limited time in Boston will find most of them convenient. I have included a couple of weekend destinations in Chapter Seven: Martha's Vineyard and Nantucket. Finally, Chapter Eight has a calendar of events, important phone numbers and websites, and how to find discounts and deals.

Quincy Market © *Greater Boston Convention & Visitors Bureau*

One: Boston in a Nutshell

A (Very) Brief History

Beantown. Hub of the Solar System. Athens of America. City on a Hill. America's Walking City. The Cradle of Liberty. Boston is called many things but not one of them can quite capture all that it is. It is impossible to ignore Boston's more than 350 years of history. We're drenched in it. The Freedom Trail offers a take on some of the more historic sites, but it's only the tip of the iceberg. It is a city that was created improbably by landfills. Back Bay, now a highly desirable part of town, was once a smelly mudflat. The project to fill it in during the late-1800s almost doubled the city's size. Actually, man, rather than nature, designed a lot of Boston's landscape. The North End and Charles Street were also mudflats. They were filled in with land from what was once Trimountaine, three hills where Beacon Hill alone remains. The State House is as tall as Beacon Hill itself once was. The Emerald Necklace, a chain of public parks designed by Frederick Law Olmsted, in part was another solution to the mudflat problem.

Presumably, most people know Boston's place in America's history. Here's a short refresher in case you need it. Boston's history as a colony started in 1630, when John Winthrop and other Puritans settled here with a charter from England. Two years later, Boston was the capital of the Massachusetts Bay Colony. (The name "Massachusetts" comes from the Native Americans who originally settled here years earlier. They were pretty much wiped out by European epidemics.) In 1684, Britain revoked the charter, but granted a new one in 1691. In 1765, things started to heat up in response to the Stamp Act, which required payment for any kind of transaction. This was a short-lived act. The colony resented Britain's unfair policies, such as more taxes and Writs of Assistance (search warrants). Five year later, the "Boston Massacre," where British troops killed five colonists in front of the Old State House really inflamed the population. In 1773, the Sons of Liberty dumped 342 crates of tea in the harbor, which became known as the "Boston Tea Party." Finally, things came to a head in 1775, when the British invaded and the American Revolution began.

After the Revolutionary War was over, Boston got back down to the business of making itself a city of firsts. The first church in the nation built by free blacks opened. The country's first abolitionist newspaper was published. The nation's first free library opened. Other firsts for Boston include the country's first telephone, and the first subway system. The list goes on and on, and Boston adds to it all the time.

Getting Your Bearings

The main neighborhoods of the city – Beacon Hill, Back Bay, Downtown, the Waterfront, Chinatown, the North End and the South End – are very accessible to each other. They each have a distinct character, but there is no real demarcation line between any of them. In the middle of all these neighborhoods are the Boston Common and the Public Garden, two of the city's best public spaces, separated only by Charles Street. The streets downtown, rather than following any logical order, instead follow the old routes of days gone by. The one-way streets, dead-ends and random turns make sense only if you're on foot. For drivers, they are just a hassle. Whenever I can, I take public transportation downtown to save myself a bunch of frustration. A little farther afield, but still accessible by the subway, are the Fenway, Charlestown, Brookline, Jamaica Plain, Roslindale, Dorchester and Roxbury. Across the Charles River is Cambridge and Harvard Square, also easily accessed by subway.

TIP: *We have long street names that we get tired of saying, so we don't. In fact, we don't like to use the complete name for anything. Here's a translation of two streets in case you ask somebody for directions and they tell you to go down Comm. Ave., past the Dunkin' Donuts, or take a right on Mass. Ave. at the Dunkin' Donuts. (One thing about Boston, all directions are given in relation to where the Dunkin' Donuts is; there are dozens in Boston.) Comm. Ave. = Commonwealth Avenue; Mass. Ave. = Massachusetts Avenue. Oh, we shorten building names, too. The "Pru" is short for the Prudential Building; the BPL is the main library; BC is Boston College, not to be confused with BU, Boston University.*

Getting Here

Most people fly into Logan International Airport (800-23-LOGAN; www.massport.com), which is two miles from town. Public transportation, via subway, bus or boat, makes getting into the city easy. A free shuttle operates between the airport and the MBTA subway (referred to as the "T"), where you can ride the Blue Line downtown and transfer to where you need to go. Cabs are plentiful. Fares start at $1.75 and cost $.30 per 1/8 mile after that. Add $1.50 for rides from the airport (the passenger is also responsible for tolls which cost $4.50). A fun way to get from the airport to the city, or vice versa, is the Airport Water Shuttle. It takes only seven minutes from the airport to Rowes Wharf. You can catch a free shuttle to the dock at any terminal. Roundtrip is $17; one-way costs $10; under 12, free. Call 617-330-422-0392.

Amtrak pulls into the North, South and Back Bay stations, 800-872-7245; www.amtrak.com. South Station, located at Atlantic Avenue and Summer Street, is the main terminal. You can easily catch a cab or take the subway from here to any downtown hotel.

Getting Around

There is really no good reason to drive in Boston, especially downtown. Unless, of course, you enjoy terrible traffic, circling like a vulture for parking spaces, and either yelling or being yelled at. Too many cars, not enough space. That's it in a nutshell. Zipcars (cars you can buy into sort of like a timeshare) are becoming very popular here because many people don't think it's worth it owning a car.

Walk or take public transportation if you can. Plus, children always think subways are an adventure in and of themselves. The destination hardly matters. I wouldn't be lying if I said I've ridden the train with my daughter back and forth just because she was happy on it. My advice if you are from out of town and have a car is to use parking garages. They are expensive but they are plentiful and convenient. Factor high parking fees ($30 a day is not unusual) into your vacation budget and save yourself a lot of stress. See if you can find an all-day lot, leave the car there and pick it up at the end of the day. If you are jumping around the city, it is still more prudent to leave the car in one spot and use the subway.

So, now you've been warned. Sometimes though, you just gotta drive. Rotaries are a painful part of driving in Boston. In theory, the driver already in the roundabout has right of way. In reality, the circles are a free-for-all, where whoever is the pushiest, wins. It seems to me every time that I am in one that I am risking life and limb. Don't assume anyone is going to yield to you.

TIP: *Five Reasons Not to Drive in Boston*
1. Apparently missing street signs. That's right. Many streets don't have signs. This is on purpose, not an accident.
2. Roads change daily. I mean this literally. One day a road is there. The next day, it's gone or goes in a new direction. This is thanks to the Big Dig (more on it below).
3. Pedestrians do not obey traffic laws. They will dart in front of your car, out of nowhere.
4. Drivers do not obey traffic laws. They will run lights. They will tailgate. Oh, and they rarely use signals.
5. Finally, you will double all your expenses by paying exorbitant parking fees if you insist on driving. Or, if you luck out and find a parking space, you'll end up feeding the meter or getting a ticket when you are delayed when trying to get change somewhere.

Public Transportation

By far the best way to get around town, other than your own two feet, is the "T," short for the Massachusetts Bay Transportation Authority (MBTA). The T is America's oldest subway line and the fourth largest in the country. It goes almost everywhere you want to go. There are four main subway lines that go downtown and out to various neighborhoods. When people talk about the T, they usually are referring to the train service, but the MBTA also runs buses and commuter trains.

The subway fare is $1.25 for adults; $.60 for kids 5-11; and free for kids under 5. A great deal is the "Visitor Passport." You can buy an unlimited travel pass for one day ($7.50); three days, ($18); or seven days ($35). This pass is good for train and bus service. Call the MBTA at 617-222-3200 for more info, and to order your passes in advance, or visit their website at www.mbta.com. Another bargain is the "Commuter Rail Family Fare." Five people, consisting of either one adult and four children, or two adults and three children, can ride for the price of two adult round-trip tickets (off-peak). The price varies depending on the destination. This makes day-trips a little cheaper for families.

Riding the T can be a little confusing for newcomers. If you remember that "Inbound" trains head toward the Park Street Station (the heart of the city) and "Outbound" trains head away from Park Street, you should be okay. To add to your confusion, although there are four colors of trains, some of them have more than one line. For example, the Green line has "B," "C," and "D" trains. Get a map and don't be afraid to ask for help!

TIP: *But Mom, why is it called the Green Line? Facts kids want to know:*
The Green Line was the first subway in America. It went from Park Street to Boylston Street in 1897. It's called the Green Line because it travels through the Emerald Necklace (details on this later).
The Red Line is called "Red" because it used to end at Harvard University, whose school color is crimson.
The Blue Line is so-called because it was the first subway in the world to travel under the ocean.
The Orange Line runs down Washington Street, which used to be named Orange Way, hence, the train's color.

Exploring on Foot

Walking is absolutely the best way to experience Boston. Of course, sometimes those little short people traveling with you don't like to walk. If practical, bring a kiddie backpack. Lots of stairs make negotiating Boston with a stroller tricky sometimes. If you are sightseeing downtown, you're never far from a subway station. Don't assume that if you are in a crosswalk, cars will stop for you. Crosswalks are more of a suggestion than anything else.

Bostonians like to creep up to the light so they can race away when it turns green. If the red and yellow lights are on at a traffic signal, this indicates that pedestrians can cross. Follow your own advice to your kids, and look both ways. Twice.

The Big Dig

Ah, the project Bostonians love to hate, otherwise know as the "Big Dig." This is another good reason to park the car somewhere and find your way on foot or train. The Central Artery/Tunnel Project (its real name), which started in 1995 and has yet to be completed, is costing billions and billions of dollars, and is America's largest public highway project to date. The main elements involve replacing Interstate 93 with an 8-to-10-lane highway tunnel under the city and extending Interstate I-90 (Mass Turnpike) to Logan Airport. The incredibly complex project (much condensed here) will result in 150 acres of new parks and open spaces. It also results in daily disruption of traffic. Detours and road closings are to be expected every hour of the day, seven days a week. Visit www.bigdig.com for the latest traffic patterns. While adults may bemoan the project and the hassles it causes, children love it. Counting cranes and backhoes should keep any kid busy. See Chapter Three for a self-guided tour of the Big Dig for really gung-ho construction lovers.

Tips for Visitors

No matter the time of year you visit, you should be prepared for anything. Snow in April, hot summery weather in October, rain one minute, gorgeous sunshine the next. None of that is unusual for Boston. You've heard it before, I'm sure, but layers are the way to go. Pack some lightweight raincoats that you can put in the bottom of your bag and hopefully never use. A sweater or sweatshirt is essential, even in summer, for those walks along the harbor or air-conditioned museums. You'll want good, sturdy shoes for exploring cobbled streets.

TIP: *What's Evacuation Day, Patriots' Day, and Bunker Hill Day anyway? They are all either state or Boston holidays. Cynics might say they are holidays so everyone can participate in or watch the St. Patrick's Day parade (Evacuation Day, March 17) and the Boston Marathon (Patriots' Day, 3rd Monday in April) but I'd never put that forth. We are just very patriotic around here. Bunker Hill Day (celebrated Friday closest to June 17) commemorates the Battle of Bunker Hill (which really occurred at Breed's Hill – don't ask, more on this later).*

Climate

As mentioned above, the weather in Boston is ever changing. There is no average temperature here, no matter what the weather forecasters say. In the summer, the temperature ranges from the 70s to the 90s degrees. Fall is anywhere between 50 to 70 degrees and winter reaches the freezing point and often dips below. Fortunately, it doesn't matter what the weather is, there's plenty to do and see even on a cold, rainy day. You'll never run out of indoor activities. If you can shelve expectations and can be flexible about outdoor plans, you'll be fine.

TIP: *Check on Boston weather by looking at the (old) John Hancock's weather lights on top of the building. Just memorize this little ditty, well known to all Boston city school children.*
Steady Blue, clear view.
Flashing Blue, clouds due.
Steady red, rain ahead.
Flashing red, snow instead (except in the summer, when flashing red means the Red Sox game is cancelled).

Two: Boston's Neighborhoods

Each of the following neighborhoods has its own distinct character and charms. Beacon Hill, with its old-world Brahmin feel is where most tourists start their visit. The Back Bay, with graceful homes and the Public Garden and Copley Square are urban meccas. The John Hancock Tower soars over the area and reflects back beautiful Trinity Church and the Boston Public Library. Nearby South End is famous as the largest neighborhood of Victorian homes in the country. While adults might find this fascinating, kids probably won't. You might head over here for lunch or dinner at one of the many restaurants.

Downtown and the Waterfront area beckon with trips out on the Boston Harbor and many historic sites. Shoppers can choose between touristy Fanueil Hall, or go to where the locals shop, Filene's Basement in Downtown Crossing. The Fenway area, of course, is home to Fenway Park and the Boston Red Sox. Many of Boston's finest cultural institutions line the "Avenue of the Arts," Huntington Avenue. Anyone with a taste for Italian should head to the North End, Boston's oldest neighborhood. Packed with restaurants, cafes and locals speaking Italian, you'll forget you're in Boston. In Charlestown, "Old Ironsides," the USS Constitution, makes its home in the Charlestown Navy Yard. Climbing the Bunker Hill Monument is worth the long climb for its fabulous views.

Jamaica Plain, Roslindale, Roxbury and Dorchester, more on the outskirts of the city, are still an important part of it. Some of the best open space in the city is at the Franklin Park and the Arnold Arboretum. Brookline and Cambridge, their own towns, are close enough to Boston to make all that they have to offer convenient destinations.

Beacon Hill

Beacon Hill, with its cobbled streets, gas lanterns and Boston Common, is the neighborhood many people see in their mind's eye when thinking about Boston. If it's your first time in the city, you'll probably spend a lot of time here, searching out old historic sites and meeting places of America's forefathers. The hill was originally called Trimountaine Hill, and was too high to build on. In the 1800s, the area was reduced, with the dirt going to create the Charles Street area and some of the North End, which were mudflats at the time. The other two hills, Pemberton and Mount Vernon, were supplanted, leaving Beacon on the top.

Massachusetts State House

The State House's gold dome gleams brightly on the hill today. As you walk around, if your kids aren't history buffs, have them look for the distinctive purple panes of glass. They result from a manufacturing defect in the 19th century, but are a beautiful flaw. Hitching posts and boot scrapers are also leftovers from an earlier era. You'll trip over the many historic sights that nestle next to modern buildings. Any time you need a break, pop into the Common or Public Garden for a breather.

African Meeting House/
Museum of Afro-American History
46 Joy Street
617-725-0022, www.afroammuseum.org
Open 10am-4pm, Mon.-Sat., Labor Day-Memorial Day; open daily 10am-4pm in the summer. Closed Thanksgiving, Christmas, and New Year's Day.
Free

Take the Red or Green Line T to Park Street Station. Walk up to Beacon Street and turn left. Take a right on Joy Street and go up the hill.
This is America's oldest standing African-American church. It was built in 1806 and was an important 19th-century center for the black community of Boston. The Meeting House was sometimes called Black Faneuil Hall. It was here that the New England Anti-Slavery Society was founded in 1832. The museum is next door to the Meeting House and offers tours and exhibits.

Benjamin Franklin Statue &
Site of America's First Public School
45 School Street
In front of Old City Hall
Take the Orange or Blue Line to State Street.
Freedom Trail Site #6

The eight-foot-tall statue of Ben Franklin was erected in 1856 and was Boston's first public portrait statue. Supposedly, one side of Franklin's face is serious, the other jovial. See if you can spot which is which. A nearby sidewalk mosaic – "City Carpet" – marks where the first public school opened (Boston Latin). Look for Ben's name, as well as those of other famous people, such as John Hancock, spelled out in glass and ceramic pieces.

Boston Common
Bordered by Tremont, Park, Boylston and Beacon streets.
Visitor's Information Center
147 Tremont Street
617-426-3115
Take any train to Park Street.
Freedom Trail Site #1

You won't see any cows on this former pasture but you will see plenty of people roaming around the 40-acre-plus green space. The country's oldest park, established in 1634, was used for grazing livestock, then for hanging criminals, and now happily is just a great place to escape to from the city sidewalks.

The Frog Pond (wading pool/ice-skating rink; see below for times) is located here, a big draw for young and old alike. A playground in the middle of the grounds is great for kids, but so is just running around the landscaped paths.

Frog Pond
Boston Common
617-635-2120
Summer: free wading pool. Winter ice-skating: adults, $3; children under 13, free. Ice-skate rentals: $5. Locker rental is $1.
Hours: Daily, 10am-9pm; open until 10pm weekends.

The Frog Pond has two delightful incarnations. In the summer it serves as a gigantic wading pool with a fountain in the middle and in winter it's the premier place to ice-skate in Boston. In November, whether it is freezing or not, the Frog Pond is turned into an ice rink, with a little help from generators. Office workers often lace up on their lunch break. Frog Pond Cottage sells snacks and hot chocolate or you can go in just to warm up.

Skating on the Frog Pond

Kim Foley MacKinnon

Boston Community Boating
21 Embankment Road on the Charles River
617-523-1038, www.community-boating.org
Junior Program season (ages 10-17):
mid-June through mid-August, weekdays 9am-3pm.
Cost: $1 for the Junior program; $100 for 2-day pass. For residents, $175 for the season for adults and $135 for youths 17-22.
Open: April-October, weekdays, 1pm-sunset; weekends, 9am-sunset
Take the Red Line T to the Charles/MGH station. Exit the station and take a left. Go over the footbridge, cross the street and cross another footbridge. Take the left-hand stairs.

This is one of the best deals in the city for children who live here, but you can also enjoy the boats as a visitor. If your older kids dream of learning to sail, this is a great place to start. A swimming certificate proving the ability to swim 75 yards is mandatory, as well as parental permission. New sailors start with five days of demonstrations, presentations as well as on-the-water instruction, and sailing with other juniors. Children can progress to skipper status and then sail by themselves. Field trips to outlying islands, the inner harbor and other activities make this an outstanding program for children. It would be wonderful even if it cost more than a buck. Adult memberships sustain the Boathouse, allowing the Junior's Program to remain such a bargain. If you are already a sailing family, take advantage of the two-day visitor's pass, available for $100 for adults (children can come as their parents' guests).

Boston Massacre Site
Devonshire and State Street
Take the Orange or Blue Line to State Street. Follow the signs.
Freedom Trail Site #10

In front of the Old State House look for a ring of cobblestones marking the spot where five colonists were killed by British soldiers during a fight that got out of hand in March, 1770. This incident was the first time blood was shed in the American Revolution.

Charles River Basin and Esplanade
Storrow Drive, Boston side of the Charles River
Take the Green Line T to Arlington Street.

The Charles River Esplanade makes a wonderful setting to walk, jog, run, in-line skate or just sit and watch the river roll on by. There are playgrounds dotted here and there on both sides of the river for kids. (Guess what? One of America's first playgrounds was on the banks of the Charles River.)

Sailing can be done at Community Boating. Shows go on all summer long at the Hatch Shell. A pool complex at one end, complete with wading pool, tennis courts, and fields offer all sorts of things to do. People line the Boston and Cambridge sides of the Charles River to watch the Head of the Charles Regatta, the Dragon Boat races and many other annual events.

TIP: *Boston's Emerald Necklace is a collection of parks designed by Frederick Law Olmsted (he also designed New York's Central Park). The jewels, which are all described elsewhere in this book, include Boston Common, the Public Garden, Commonwealth Mall, the Back Bay Fens, the Riverway, Olmsted Park, Jamaica Pond, Arnold Arboretum and Franklin Park. Go to www.emerald-necklace.org for more info.*

Hatch Memorial Shell

Storrow Drive
617-727-9547, ext. 450
Take the Green Line T to Arlington Street.

Warm weather brings concerts and events to the half-shell shaped concert hall on the banks of the Charles River. The giant Art Deco clamshell was erected in 1940; prior concerts had been happening in the same spot since 1910. You may have seen the Boston Pops perform the famed Fourth of July show here on TV or even braved the crowds to see it live. It's an impressive sight watching the fireworks bursting over the Charles River, with the Pops as the background music. Free movies on Friday nights during the summer are a special treat for the whole family. We've seen the "Wizard of Oz" here, which definitely beats a drive-in in my book. Other events occur throughout the year, including free rock concerts sponsored by radio stations and classical fare as well. Get here early with a blanket to claim a spot for popular events.

King's Chapel & Burying Ground

Corner of School and Tremont streets
617-227-2125, www.kings-chapel.org
Open: 10am-5pm; closed Mondays.
Admission: Free for children;
adults requested to make a donation.
Take the Orange or Blue Line to State Street.
Freedom Trail Site #5

No colonists would sell land to the Royal Governor to build a Church of England church in 1688, so he ordered one be built on the already existing burying ground. The church was too small for the congregation by 1749, so a new one was designed by

Peter Harrison, America's first architect, in 1754. This was your last stop if you were to be hanged in Boston Common. The burying ground is the oldest in the city of Boston.

Massachusetts State House
Beacon Street
617-727-3676, www.state.ma.us/sec/trs
Open for free tours Mon.-Fri., 10am-4pm.
Take any train to the Park Street Station. Walk up Park Street.
Freedom Trail Site #2

What's old is new in Boston. You'll easily find your way to the gold-domed topped "new" State House, designed by Charles Bulfinch, and built in 1798. It's the oldest building on Beacon Hill and houses the state government. Visitors on the 45-minute tour can see the Hall of Flags and the Senate and House Chambers. (The "old" State House was built in 1713.) Look for the "Sacred Cod" hanging in the House Gallery, representing the importance of the fishing industry to the city.

Museum of Science/Omni Theater/ Planetarium/Computer Museum
Science Park
617-723-2500, www.mos.org
Open daily, 9am-5pm, with extended hours on Friday until 9pm; summer schedule: July 5-Labor Day,
9am-7pm; Closed Thanksgiving and Christmas.
Admission: $13, adults; $10, children 3-11; under 3, free.
Mugar Omni Theater,
Planetarium and Laser Shows are extra.
Take the Lechmere Green Line T to the Science Park stop. The Museum is 200 yards from the station.

The Children's Museum is always the obvious choice to take the kids, and although there is plenty for children to do, it can be a little tedious for adults. I far prefer taking my five-year-old daughter to the Museum of Science, where there are exhibits and activities that we both can enjoy. On a recent visit, we first went to the children's section called the "Discovery Room." Exhibits range from dinosaur bone replicas that the kids can play with to a large aquarium filled with guinea pigs. There's also an arts activity center, water table to splash in, climbing structure and more. In one section of the Discovery Room, there is an infant-only area.

Out in the Museum proper, one of our old favorites is a space shuttle you can climb into and pretend to blast off. A fun exhibit on the physics of playgrounds explains why you go up while your friend goes down on the teeter-totter. The Museum of Science can easily provide an entire day's worth of fun and is a great place to go when it's rainy. The cafeteria offers better-than-average food and there is a huge gift shop with unique souvenirs. Visitors and locals both enjoy this museum.

For that virtual feeling you can only get with IMAX, visit the Mugar Omni Theater. This is the largest movie screen in Boston, at five stories high. Sit in the eye of a tornado or climb Mt. Everest. Also at the Museum of Science is the Charles Hayden Planetarium, where you can see an amazingly realistic night sky or take in one of their special programs that change every six months.

New England Holocaust Memorial
Located on Congress Street near Faneuil Hall
Friends of the New England Holocaust Memorial
126 High Street
617-457-0755, www.nehm.org
Take the Blue or Orange Line T to State Street.

Six 54-foot-tall glass towers, etched with six million numbers, makes a sobering memorial to the Holocaust victims. The six towers are meant to represent the six main Nazi death camps, the six million Jews who died and a menorah, all at once. Smoke rises from embers of six dark chambers named for the main death camps. The towers are lit from within at night. They are an excellent opportunity for parents to discuss an ugly chapter of history with their children, who will no doubt spot the towers if you are near downtown and Faneuil Hall.

Old Corner Bookstore
Corner of School and Washington streets
617-367-4004, www.historicboston.org
Open daily, Mon.-Fri., 9am-5:30 pm; Sat., 9am-5pm; Sunday, noon-5pm.
Take the Orange or Blue Line to State Street.
Freedom Trail Site #7

This one-time home and apothecary shop, built in 1712, gave way to a publishing house in 1832. The Scarlet Letter, Walden, and the magazine *Atlantic Monthly* were all published here. Charles Dickens and Ralph Waldo Emerson were frequent visitors. The famous site almost was demolished to make way for a parking lot but concerned citizens stepped in and saved the day, as often happens when a piece of local history is under threat in Boston. Today, *The Boston Globe* is the latest tenant and sells books about Boston and New England.

Old South Meeting House
310 Washington Street
617-482-6439, www.oldsouthmeetinghouse.org
Open daily, 9:30am-5pm
Admission: Adults, $5; children 18 and under, $1
Take the Orange or Blue Line to State Street.
Freedom Trail Site #8

This is where it all began. At least, this is where the famous Boston Tea Party began. In 1773, 5,000 colonialists, angry over taxes and the Boston Massacre, raced out of the meeting hall down to the harbor and dumped three shiploads of tea into the water. Of course, it took a couple more years and acts of defiance before the British tried to bring these upstart colonialists in line. They didn't succeed. The Meeting House was built in 1729 and was the largest building in Boston at the time. Come by for a re-enactment of the famous debates.

Old State House
Corner of State and Washington streets
617-720-3290, www.bostonhistory.org
Open daily, 9am-5pm; closed New Year's Day, Thanksgiving and Christmas.
Admission: Adults, $5; children 6-18, $1.
Take the Orange or Blue Line to State Street. Follow the signs. The station is under the Old State House.
Freedom Trail Site #9

The 1713 building was at first home to the British government; later it was the first place the Declaration of Independence was heard in Massachusetts. Every July 4th, the Declaration is read from the same balcony. The Old State House is Boston's oldest public building. The lion and the unicorn sculptures are leftovers from the British Crown. Look for the cobblestone circle outside the building marking the Boston Massacre site.

At one time there was a plan to move the Old State House to the Chicago's World Fair. Of course, no self-respecting Bostonian was going to allow that to happen. In 1879, the Antiquarian Club was formed to stop it from happening. The club evolved into the Bostonian Society and started a museum of Boston's history. They also operate a library, heavy on 18th and 19th century artifacts and papers, open to museum visitors, across the street.

Park Street Church & Granary Burying Ground

Park and Tremont streets
Open July-August from 9:30am-3:30pm; in winter, by appointment.
Services open to the public Sundays at 8:30am, 11am, 4 & 6 pm.
617-523-3383, www.parkstreet.org
Take any train to the Park Street Station.
Freedom Trail Sites #3 & #4

This church, founded in 1809, is still vibrant and well attended. Its 217-foot steeple was long the first landmark seen by travelers to the city. Many anti-slavery speeches occurred here in the 1800s. The kids might be interested to find out that "My Country 'Tis of Thee" was first sung by the children's choir here.

The Granary Burying Ground, next to the church, holds the remains of Samuel Adams, Paul Revere and John Hancock, among many other famous revolutionaries. "Mother Goose," really Elizabeth Vergoose, is also buried here. It's open daily from 9am-5pm (in winter, it closes at 3pm).

Take 10 – Tadpole Playground

Right in the heart of Boston Common is a much-needed respite from all your traipsing about, the aptly named Tadpole Playground, located next to the Frog Pond. After climbing up and down the hills of Beacon Hill or shopping at Downtown Crossing, head here to rest your weary feet. The scenery and people watching can't be beat. Grab lemonade or fried dough from one of the many vendors around while the children climb. This playground was completely redone in 2003 and kids will love petting the two frog statues that stand sentry at the entrance.

The Back Bay

It really was a bay, part of the Charles River. Actually, it was more of a swamp than a bay and was considered a health hazard. In the 1800s, it was filled in and developed over a period of 30 years. It's something to think about when you are walking around the area, where the only hazards now are to your credit cards. Today, you'll find Newbury Street fun for window-shopping, Copley Square a mecca for workers on their lunch break, and tourists gazing up at the tall towers and beautiful architecture all around. Commonwealth Avenue Mall is a long green walkway filled with statues and on either side, beautiful. The Public Garden is the area's contemplative spot, while the Esplanade hosts the louder events, like the Pops concert on July fourth.

Swan Boats

Boston Public Central Library

666 Boylston Street
617-536-5400, www.bpl.org
Open Mon.-Thurs., 9am-9pm; Fri.-Sat., 9am-5pm; closed Sunday.
Take the Green Line T to the Copley Square stop.

It's hard to know where to begin with the main Boston Public Library, so we'll start with all the firsts. The library, which was founded in 1848 and opened in 1854, was the first free library open to the public in the United States. It was also the first to allow patrons to borrow materials; the first to institute a branch system; and the first to set aside a separate room for children. In addition to its more than 6 million books, it's stocked with sculptures, murals and paintings by famous artists, making a tour of the building a pleasure. Children love the funky wrought-iron lanterns outside, and the two giant marble lions that greet visitors on the main staircase.

Really, entering the library from the main entrance hall may make you think you are entering a museum with all the works of art. Free tours are given October through May, Sundays at 2pm; Mondays at 2:20pm; Tuesdays and Thursdays at 6 pm; and Fridays and Saturdays at 11am. Don't dismiss this out of hand unless you have really antsy kids. Children are usually fascinated by all the beautiful frescoes and sculptures. If you need a breath of fresh air, visit the lovely inner courtyard in the attached McKim building.

The amount of activities at the library – free activities – is another facet that makes it a treasure. On Friday mornings at 10:15am there is Kids' Cinema. Movies such as "Curious George Rings the Bell" or "The Little Red Hen" entertain preschoolers. Puppet shows and other special activities are scheduled throughout the year. One final note for locals, if you don't already know: The library has free or discounted passes for many museums in town. All you need is a library card. Each Boston library has different passes. Call around in advance to see if you can get what you want. I pick up a schedule each month to see what's happening at the main library. Once, my daughter got a free dance lesson from a noted local performer. All we had to do was sign up! Two restaurants call the library home. Read about them in Chapter Five.

Colonnade Hotel Rooftop Pool
120 Huntington Avenue
800-962-3030; 617-424-7000, www.colonnadehotel.com
Open Memorial Day-Labor Day, 9am-6pm
Admission: $40 for the day: $20 after 3pm. Changes seasonally. Call to confirm.
Take the Green Line to the Hynes/ICA stop. Follow signs to Huntington Avenue.

This is one of things that wouldn't normally occur to a parent: bringing your child to a fancy hotel for the day to hang out. But this is one of Boston's summertime treats. The rooftop pool has an excellent view of the city and is a bargain at the price when the backyard plastic wading pool won't do. A snack bar has a limited menu. Towels are provided. There are even showers and a changing area. Parents will have to serve as lifeguards.

Copley Square
Boylston Street
Take the Green Line T to Copley Square.

Copley Square, a wonderful public space surrounded by the Boston Public Library, Trinity Church, the John Hancock Building and Boylston Street, is always a busy hub of activity. Take a minute to relax in the plaza while the children visit the Tortoise and Hare statues or chase after pigeons. The large fountain offers a soothing counterpoint to the bustle of the city around you. In the summer, there's a farmer's market where you can buy fresh fruits and vegetables. Check out the Bostix kiosk and see what half-price tickets are available for that night. Any number of restaurants and fast food joints line Boylston Street. One street over is tony Newbury Street where you can window shop. Look for a Hello Kitty store and Niketown.

FAO Schwartz Bear
440 Boylston Street
Take the Green Line to Copley Square.
Good for a photo op. The store went bankrupt, but the bear remains, for now.

Kim Foley MacKinnon

Institute of Contemporary Art
955 Boylston Street
617-266-5152, www.icaboston.org
Open: Tues. & Fri., noon-5pm; Thurs., noon-9pm; weekends, 11am-5pm.
Admission: $7, adults; under 12, free. Free Thursdays after 5pm.
Take the Green Line (B, C, or D) to the Hynes Convention Center/ICA stop.

The Institute of Contemporary Art has an ever-changing series of exhibitions, which means you'll see something new every time you visit. For now, the museum is on Boylston Street but it is scheduled to open in larger quarters on the waterfront at Fan Pier in 2005. The whole waterfront area is under construction, like half of Boston it seems, but should be fabulous when finished. Whenever we visit, photography exhibits always draw my daughter in.

An interesting program they have, Vita Brevis, might interest the family as you do other exploring through Boston. The program sponsors an artist to create a temporary work of art in the city. One example is an exhibit of Icelandic lava at the Fan Pier in Boston Harbor that was installed from August through September of 2001. Check out their website to see what's up when you are visiting.

John Hancock Tower
200 Clarendon Street
Take the Green Line T to Copley Square.

Sadly, the 60th floor observatory is no longer open to the public. The terrorist events of September 11, 2001, made safety a higher priority, necessitating its closing. Although the view from the top may be missed, the I.M. Pei building itself is better admired from afar. Seen from different points in the city, an optical illusion makes it look thin as a sheet of paper. It's a good way to keep your bearings getting around town. When it was near completion in the early 1970s, a miscalculation of the stress of wind on the 60-story building made Bostonians run for cover as windows fell out. Don't worry. They've all been replaced! For a great view of the Hancock, go to the Skywalk at the Prudential.

Make Way for Ducklings Statues
Boston Public Garden
Take the Red or Green Line T to Park Street.

If you live in Boston, you've probably read the book to your kids at least a few dozen times. If you're not from around here or somehow just never picked up the classic "Make Way for Ducklings," by Robert McClosky, you should. And then bring the children to the bronze sculptures of Mrs. Mallard and her brood marching along. They're big enough for the children to climb on, which usually proves an irresistible photo op for all shutterbugs. A charming event is the Duckling Parade on Mother's Day, when children dress up as ducks and march through the streets.

Mapparium & Fountain at the Christian Science Center
175 Huntington Avenue
617-450-3790, www.marybakereddylibrary.org
Open Tues. Wed, Sat. Sun., 10am-5pm; Thurs. & Fri., until 9pm;
closed major holidays.
Admission: $5; children 6-17, $3; under 6, free.
Fountain on in the summer. Free
Take the Green Line T to Hynes Auditorium. Take a left on Massachusetts Ave and go three blocks.

The Christian Science Publication Society Building sounds daunting but the huge complex on Mass. Ave. has a lot to offer children. Actually, a new research library, the Mary Baker Eddy Library for the Betterment of Humanity (another mouthful) opened in the fall of 2002 and offers interactive exhibits. Eddy was the founder of Christian Science and the Christian Science Monitor newspaper. The Hall of Ideas details great ideas throughout history. Another exhibit focuses on the Christian Science Monitor and how it produces its news.

What interests children most are probably the enormous fountain outside (670 x 100 feet) and the Mapparium, a gigantic stained glass globe that you can walk through. It's 30 feet in diameter and quite beautiful. It's a look at world geography as it was in 1935; updating it would be a daunting task. It doesn't matter though, walking through is pretty neat. You can whisper to each other across the room and it will sound like you are standing next to each other because of the acoustics.

Summertime, besides drawing in kids to splash in the fountain, brings all sorts of activities outside. What they call "Summer Soulstice" is a series of free events on Tuesdays at either 11am or noon. There may be participatory drumming and balloon sculpture one week and perhaps a presentation by the Huntington Theatre Company the next. The programs are about an hour-and-a-half long and the variety is wonderful. They even have a rain site, inside the Sunday school building.

Public Garden
Charles Street, across from Boston Common.
617-635-7383
Take the Green Line to Arlington Street.

The Public Garden, home to the Swan Boats and the duckling statues, is a lot more than a delightful play spot for children. It was established in 1837 and is the oldest public botanical garden in the country. Hundreds of species of trees and flowers abound in the beautiful park. It's a luxurious 24 acres, right in the heart of the city. Activity is pretty low-key. Take a walk over the world's smallest suspension bridge. No biking or skating is permitted or laying on much of the grassy areas. Children love to feed the many ducks in the lagoon and watch the Swan Boats peddle by, but for more to do, head to the Common.

Skywalk at the Prudential Tower

800 Boylston Street, 50th floor
617-859-0648
Open daily 10am-10pm
Admission: Adults, $7; under 10, $4
Take the Green Line T to the Prudential Stop.

You can take a break from shopping, as if you could actually do any with your kids anyway, and head up to the 50th floor in the Prudential Tower for a 360-degree view of Boston. It's great on a clear day and now that the Hancock Tower is closed, this is the best view of the city, in the city. Children do like to see the world reduced in scale and are often content to just gaze out in wonder how high they are. There are a few interactive displays around, but if you are looking for more than a bird's-eye view, save your money for something else.

Swan Boats

Public Garden Lagoon
617-522-1966, www.swanboats.org
Open: mid-April through mid-September from 10am-5pm
Admission: Adults, $2.50; children 2-15; $1
Take the Red or Green Line T to Arlington Street Station.

This is one thing that everybody should do at least once for the sheer enjoyment value. Floating though the lagoon for 15 minutes in a giant swan peddled by foot has to be one of life's little pleasures. Oh, and the kids love it too. The Swan Boats have been in service for over a hundred years, operated by the Paget family, and are one more thing that makes Boston such a special

place. Where else can you ride a swan in the middle of the city?
Remember to bring along some bread to feed the ducks that
follow you around. They expect it as their due.

Tortoise & Hare Statues
Copley Square

Keep an eye out for these two. They are near the finish line of the
Boston Marathon and serve as a tribute to all who run, no matter
how they place in the race. Kids love to climb on them. Let them
play while you relax on benches by the fountain. Don't think
you'll get anywhere near them during the actual m though.
Copley Square is packed with spectators for the annual event in
April.

Trinity Church
Copley Square
617-536-0944, www.trinitychurch.org
Open daily, 8am-6pm
Admission: Free, but $4 donation requested
Take the Green Line T to Copley Square stop.

With kids in tow, you probably wouldn't make this a destination
alone, but it's easy to pop in if you are in the area seeing other
sights. Take a break from walking around Copley Square or
shopping and look into this national architectural landmark. The
Romanesque-style church was built in 1877 and is still a working
church. Stop by on Fridays in the school year at noon to hear free
organ recitals.

Take 10 – Clarendon Street Playground
At the corner of Clarendon Street and Commonwealth Avenue.
This is a top-notch playground, maintained faithfully by a
neighborhood committee. Toys for all to use are a friendly touch.

It's just a block from busy Newbury Street. If you tire of the playground, a walk on Commonwealth Mall is soothing. You should know that many local preschools and schools use the playground, so it can get crowded.

Downtown & the Waterfront

For convenience's sake, I am lumping these areas together, although they really cover a lot of area. With the kids you'll be focusing on specific sites, many of which are clustered together. You'll find more than government offices in Government Center. City Hall Plaza is packed with festivals and events in the summer. The kids will love Faneuil Hall, with all its shopping and hoopla. LongWharf has always been the center of the harbor, and in this area you'll find tons of sightseeing boats ready to take you out to the water. The New England Aquarium and the Boston Tea Party Ship and Museum bring people flocking to the area.

Boston Harbor Cruises
One Long Wharf
877-733-9425; 617-227-4321, www.bostonharborcruises.com
The ticket office is located on the wharf and the cruises leave from here. Take the T to State Street Station (via the Orange or Blue line) and follow signs to Long Wharf.

Boston Harbor Cruises, or BHC, offers a bunch of different options for spending time on the water. You can take their high-speed catamaran to watch whales, visit the Boston Harbor Islands, tour the harbor, zip over to Provincetown on a fast ferry or be entertained on a musical cruise. Here's a dirty, little secret that no one tells you though: Many people get seasick, even on a calm sea! If you think you or your children might be one of them, take care. There is medicine you can take to combat seasickness, but it must be taken well in advance (usually four hours) of getting on the water. That said, here is a rundown on BHC's offerings.

High-Speed Catamaran Whale Watches
Summer schedule: Departs Long Wharf 10am & noon weekdays; 8:30am, 10:30am, 12:30pm & 2:30pm, weekends; sunset cruise, 5:30pm on weekends. Call for spring, fall & holiday cruises.
Admission: Adults, $30; children, $24.

If you are crazy about whales, you will definitely want to do this. If you get seasick or your kids get easily bored, this is not for you. The three-hour roundtrip consists mostly of getting out to Stellwagen Bank – home of humpback, minke, and finback whales – and back. BHC promises that if you don't see a whale, they'll give you a free ticket to try again but that rarely happens. On a perfect September day, our family and some friends got to see "Glowstick" a young female whale, strut her stuff. She flipped, splashed, and smacked the water with her tail to the delight of everyone onboard. A naturalist from the Whale Center of New England narrates during each whale watch, which is how we learned Glowstick's name. Bring something for the kids to do when they are tired of looking out of the windows. It's a good idea to bring a picnic along too, although there is a snack bar onboard.

Provincetown Fast Ferry
The ferry runs May-October. It departs Long Wharf at 9am and returns at 4pm, Mon.-Thurs. On Fri.-Sun., additional runs from Boston are at 2pm and 6:30pm. Additional returns from Provincetown are at 4pm and 8:30pm.
Price for Roundtrip: Adults, $58, under 12, $48.

Just going for the 90-minute ride in this high-speed catamaran is enough of an adventure for lots of people, never mind Provincetown. Perks include a concierge who can book bike rentals for you and free admission to the Whydah Museum (filled with pirate artifacts) in Provincetown where you dock. The ferry is a little pricey, but it's a great way to avoid the hassles of driving to P-Town and makes for a fun day trip.

Harbor Islands State Park

Ferry service is available from Long Wharf (next to the New England Aquarium). Bay State Cruises (617-723-7800) transports passengers to Georges Island, where you can catch a free water taxi to the other islands.
www.bostonislands.org
Take the Red Line T to South Station. It's then a 10-minute walk down Atlantic Avenue, right past the Boston Harbor Hotel
Ferry service is every hour, on the hour, from 10am-5pm, weather permitting. Call to make sure it's running if the weather seems iffy to you.
Cost: $8 for adults; $6 for children 12 and under.
45 minutes by ferry from downtown.

This is a great all-day activity if the weather is nice and you need a break from the hustle and bustle of the city. In less than an hour, and a fun and informative hour at that (park rangers narrate on the way over), you are transported to one of Boston's best offerings. This state park has got it all: spectacular views, history, peace and quiet. An added bonus is that there are no cars here, you don't need to worry about little ones getting run over Pack a picnic, sunscreen and a Frisbee, and you'll have a memory in the making. You can visit others on a free water taxi. Camping is available on certain islands. Advance reservations required.

Georges Island, with 28 acres, is the park's centerpiece, and where the ferry docks. There's a visitor's center, dock, picnic grounds, snack bar, toilets and a beach (no swimming though). Fort Warren was built here between 1833 and 1869. It is a National Historic Landmark and was used as a prison for Confederate soldiers in the Civil War. Exploring the fort is an adventure in itself. Tours are sometimes offered by park rangers. Call for times.

My family and a few friends with children went to Georges Island in the summer and everyone loved it. The ferry alone is a big treat for younger children. Don't be afraid of lugging a big cooler (with plenty of water). A nice touch on the island is that at the dock you'll find free wooden wheelbarrows available to haul your stuff (or your kids) around. A word of warning, except for inside the fort, there is not a lot of shade here, so an umbrella is a good idea to give you a break from the sun.

Boston Fire Museum
344 Congress Street
617-482-1344, www.bostonfiremuseum.com
Open Saturdays April-November, noon-4pm.
Free
Take the Red Line to South Station. Walk up Atlantic Avenue to Congress.

The little 1899 firehouse makes for a charming visit if you can time it right. Open only in the summer for a few hours on Saturdays means you have to plan in advance, although if you can get someone to call you back, you might be able to schedule a better time for you to visit. Inside the museum, there are antique fire equipment and photos. Children can play with and climb on some of the equipment. This is a stop only if your children can't get enough of fire engines.

Boston Light &
Little Brewster Island
Boston Harbor
617-223-8666, www.bostonislands.org
Open June-September, Thursday (10am from Fan Pier); Friday-Sunday (10am & 2pm from Columbia Point)
Admission: Adults, $27; children 6-12, $17; under 5, free.

Boston Light is, you guessed it, America's oldest light station. Your admission gets you a three-and-a-half hour ranger guided tour. This includes an hour narration on the boat, where you'll spot three other lighthouses on the way to Little Brewster Island. You spend an hour-and-a-half on the island itself, which is less than two acres in size, and you can meet the last official light keepers in the country. The original lighthouse was built in 1716, but the British mostly destroyed it in the Revolutionary War. It was rebuilt in 1783. It stands 102 feet tall and you can climb up to the top on your visit (up 76 stairs and two ladders). The US Coast Guard, which runs the lighthouse, was all set to automate it in 1990, like every other lighthouse in the country, when preservation groups protested (we're so good at protesting here!). So, the Coast Guard mans the lighthouse. If you can swing it, this really is a fascinating tour and you can't beat the view from the lighthouse. Here's a piece of trivia for the kids: the beacon can be seen for 27 miles.

Boston Tea Party Ship & Museum
Congress Street Bridge
617-338-1773, www.bostonteapartyship.com
Take the Red Line to South Station. Go toward the water on Atlantic Avenue, then take a left on Congress Street.

At press time, the ship was closed due to a fire in the summer of 2001, but it is slated to be repaired and re-open in 2005. You'll have to call to find out. If you're anywhere near the Museum Wharf, you'll spot the ship. Brig Beaver II is a recreation of the smallest of three ships that colonists boarded in that famous December night of 1773. Dressed as Native Americans, the colonists, or "Sons of Liberty," dumped more than 300 crates of tea into the harbor as a protest of unfair taxes.

Children's Museum
300 Congress Street
617-426-8855, www.bostonkids.org
Open daily 10am-5pm; Friday until 9pm.
Admission: Adults, $9; children 2-15, $7; under 1, free.
Friday nights admission is $1 per person from 5-9pm.
Take the Red Line to South Station. Walk around the Federal Reserve
Building and down to the water. The museum is behind the giant Hood Milk
Bottle.

Three levels of interactive activities and exhibits can keep
children busy all day long. Families with small children (under
three) should head straight for the Smith Family Playspace on the
second floor. There is even a protected infant area with
appropriate toys. An outstanding feature is the Family Resource
Room where moms can go nurse and parents can catch up on all
the latest parenting information in the library. You can even grab
a cup of coffee here, which you might need to keep up with your
kids.

Out of the toddler area there are many options for the kids to
explore. My daughter likes to go up to Grandparents' Attic on the
fourth floor to play dress up. Nearby is the Arthur's World
exhibit, a recreation of that famous aardvark's house, school and
tents (for when he goes camping). There is also a stage on this
floor, with shows taking place periodically. Tickets are free but
limited, so you should pick them up when you first come in the
museum. The Supermercado is also very popular, where kids can
pretend they are at a Latin American supermarket. Older kids will
like the rock-climbing structure (adults can climb too!). There are
many other exhibits and you probably won't be able to visit them
all in one day.

If it is warm out, you can have lunch outside at the giant Hood
Milk Bottle, which sells snacks (don't forget to get your hand

stamped when you leave the museum so you can go back in). If you brought your own picnic, you can go to the Lunch Room on the first floor, or, (you've got to love this) there is a McDonald's adjacent to the museum.

Chinatown

Boston's Chinatown is the third largest in the country, although you'd never guess it. It is very small but packed tight and located right next to the Downtown Crossing shopping area. Go to the Chinatown T stop on the Green Line, if you want to hop out and explore. Kids will probably enjoy the Chinatown gates, standing 36 feet tall, at the entrance to the area. Four marble Chinese dogs, weighing in at 3,000 pounds each, stand guard. They were a gift from Taiwan. Eating and shopping are the main tourist activities here. Look for the phone booths topped with colorful pagodas.

Custom House Tower

3 McKinley Square
617-310-6300
Tours given daily at 10am & 4pm, except Sat. when there is no 10am tour. No tours in inclement weather.
Free, but donation requested.
Take the Blue Line to the Aquarium stop.

The Custom House Tower is officially called the Marriott Custom House, which means what you think it means. It wasn't always so. The Custom House was built in 1847 and when the 30-foot tower was added in 1915, it made it the city's first skyscraper. The beautiful clock tower is often photographed and a familiar sight to many. The Marriott Vacation Club International refurbished the Custom House, doing such a good job in preserving it, while also turning it into a luxury hotel, that it won a 1999 National Preservation Honor Award from the

National Trust for Historic Preservation. Today, you can take a guided tour, providing the weather cooperates.

Downtown Crossing
Intersection of Washington Street with Winter and Summer streets.
Take any inbound train to the Downtown Crossing or Park Street T stops.

Famous Filene's Basement and dozens of other stores are located in this pedestrian-only shopping area downtown. Maybe your kids like shopping (mine doesn't) but all the bustling activity outside is always entertaining. You can always take your children to the annual wedding dress sale at the Basement as a lesson on how NOT to behave.

Faneuil Hall Marketplace & Quincy Market
Congress Street
617-523-1300, www.faneuilhallmarketplace.com
Take the Green Line T to Government Center. Cross City Hall Plaza.
Freedom Trail Site # 11

Faneuil Hall (FAN-yul) was built in 1742 as a public meeting and marketplace. Quincy Market was built next door in the 1800s, as more space was needed. Boston picked up its "Cradle of Liberty" nickname from the goings-on here because of the many important speeches about freedom that occurred in the Colonial era. Today, the area is a major tourist draw, packed with stores and restaurants. Look for the four-foot copper grasshopper weathervane on top of Faneuil Hall. (Why a grasshopper? No one knows.)

Two stories of eateries and shops entice young and old alike into Quincy Market. This is a good quick-food stop, but you'll be among lots of tourists. Artists and street performers entertain outside.

HarborWalk

The HarborWalk is a work-in-progress. Construction on the waterfront, to include a new convention center, hotels, shops and museum is eagerly awaited by the city. For now, it runs from Long Wharf to the fish pier. Along the route you'll find the Aquarium, Rowes Wharf, the Boston Tea Party Museum and ship and Museum Wharf, where the Children's Museum is located.

Haymarket
Around the corner from Quincy Market.
Open Friday & Saturday
Take the Green or Orange Line T to the Haymarket stop.

On Fridays and Saturdays you might be drawn to the loud commotion near Quincy Market. There's nothing wrong. It's just the loud vendors at Haymarket trying to entice buyers to buy fruit, fish and vegetables at Boston's outdoor food market. This market has been here for 200 years, believe or not. If your kids want a lesson in how haggling really works, pop on by. Hold on tight to your kids here – it is always packed with jostling customers and they're not too polite if you get in their way (beware of bad language, too!). One more warning for both you and the kids: no touching allowed. What you see is what you get.

Liberty Fleet of Tall Ships
Ticket office: 67 Long Wharf
617-742-0333, www.libertyfleet.com
June-September: Daily sails at noon, 3pm, and 6pm. Sun. brunch sail, 11am.
Daily sails, $30 for adults; $18 under 12. Brunch: $45, adults; $25, under 12.
Departs from Long Wharf.

There is nothing like sailing around Boston Harbor in one of these beautiful tall ships that come to visit in the summer. The

Liberty Clipper and the Liberty both offer two-and-a-half hour tours where you can relax on deck or join in and help the crew with hoisting the sails. Drinks are available to buy on board, but bring your own snacks. Anyone who truly longs to be on the water won't be able to pass up the 18th century replicas of schooners.

New England Aquarium & Simon's 3D IMAX Theater
Central Wharf
617-973-5200, www.neaq.org
Mon.-Fri., 9am-5pm; Sat.-Sun., 9am-6 pm.
Admission: Adults, $15.95; children 3-11, $8.95; under 3, free
Take the Orange or Blue line to the State Street/Aquarium stop.

We always find the Aquarium a soothing, mysterious place to be. We talk a little more softly in here. The darkened halls highlight the animals swimming in tanks. Our all-time favorite is the giant ocean tank that is the centerpiece of the museum. The 200,000-gallon tank, formally named the Caribbean Coral Reef Exhibit, is a 24-foot-deep reef filled with caves, reefs, sharks, turtles and hundreds of tropical fish. A winding ramp leads up around the tank and visitors can peek in windows as they stroll up four stories to the top. Smaller children will love the tide pool exhibit where they can get wet and hold starfish. Special activities such as playing with sea lions are available (for additional cost). The Aquarium also offers whale watches and harbor tours.

Simon's IMAX Theater
Shows daily, additional shows Fri. and Sat. evenings
Admission: Adults, $8.95; children ages 3-11, $6.95

If you worry that our 24/7 media culture has rendered the next generation jaded to visual wonder, you are in for a happy surprise when you bring them to the New England Aquarium's new giant-screen theater. The beautiful 300-seat theater occupies its own building adjacent to the Aquarium, which it dwarfs with its many stories-tall screen. But the effect of the films – which take up aquatic themes – is much more than bigger-is-better. This is as close to scuba diving as most of us are going to get.

Some of the IMAX films screened at the Aquarium are shot with 3-D technology, which has the effect of making the images on the 84-foot screen appear as if they are floating just inches in front of your face. The effect is so real that younger children often wave their hands in front of them, attempting to reach out and touch what they see. Older children and adults will also be spellbound, especially those with an interest in wildlife or an adventurous spirit.

Lion's Mane Jelly © *Norman Katz*

Any child who is old enough to sit still and wear glasses will enjoy the spectacle. And grown ups who can't imagine a school of ocean mackerel capable of making them gasp – think again. Highly recommended.

Take 10: Christopher Columbus Park

This playground, with its structure shaped like a ship, is located right on Commercial Wharf. It's the perfect place for the kids to pretend they are sailing off to sea. You can sit and watch the action in the harbor or wander over to Rose Kennedy's Rose Garden. There's lots of shade and a fountain to splash around in if it's hot. Joe's American Bar & Grill is next to the park if you want a bite (kid's menu available).

Fenway

The Fenway, home to the Boston Red Sox and the Museum of Fine Arts, is sometimes called the Avenue of the Arts. This area really grew up in the early 1900s, when many institutions started building over here. Huntington Avenue, the main stretch, has museums and theatres vying for your attention in this cultural center. (You'll find theatres listed in Chapter Four.) Fenway Park was built in 1912 in Kenmore Square. On game days, the area is a mob scene before and after games, and so is the "B" train on the Green Line T. You can't miss the famous double-sided neon CITGO billboard if you're in the area.

Back Bay Fens

The Back Bay Fens is part of Boston's Emerald Necklace. Its previous life was that of a marsh, which was drained and filled in, and then turned into parkland. It is fun to walk through the Victory Gardens, the nation's oldest remaining WWII gardens. There is also a rose garden, absolutely stunning in bloom, and myriad pathways to explore. This is a good place to wander around if you need a break from the nearby museums and some fresh air.

Fenway Park & Tours
4 Yawkey Way
617-226-6666, www.redsox.mlb.com
Take the Green Line T to the Fenway Station.
Tickets: Start at $18. There are special discount days when you can get a ticket for as little as $9. Call for details.
Tours: May-August, Monday-Friday, on the hour, 9am-4pm; last tour three hours before home games. Meet at the Souvenir Store on Yawkey Way. Adults, $10; under 14, $8.

Built in 1912, Fenway Park is the last original ballpark in the American League. Replete with yore and historical character, Fenway is a piece of Americana, but this destination is more an older kid activity and then only for those really interested in baseball.

I recommend doing a behind-the-scenes tour if you are around in the summer. You get to see the pressroom, the 600 Club, privates suites, and best of all, you'll get on the field. You can even touch the "Green Monster" and sit in the dugout. The tour is about an hour.

TIP: *At night, look for the CITGO sign flashing in Kenmore Square. Through the years plans to take down the sign have met with such protest from Bostonians that it is sure to stay a familiar icon for decades to come.*

Isabella Stewart Gardner Museum
280 The Fenway
617-566-1401, www.gardenermusuem.org
Open Tues.-Sun., 11am-5pm. Closed Thanksgiving & Christmas.
Admission: Adults, $10 ($11 on weekends); under 18, free.
Take the Green Line T to the Museum of Fine Arts stop.

The Gardner Museum, a wonderful place left exactly as it was when Isabella Stewart Gardner was alive, as per her wishes, can be great to explore with children. It might not seem that way at first, though. Gardner designed the museum as a Venetian palace and opened three floors to the public in 1903. She lived on the fourth floor until her death in 1924. It is a smaller museum and the rooms circle the garden courtyard, which always has blooming plants (a welcome sight in the winter).

Pick up the family guides available at the info desk on your way in. One is called "Eyes on Fenway Court." You'll explore the beautiful inner courtyard of the museum and look for various works of art with clues like this from the guide: "I am a dolphin made out of stone. I am a twin. I am not alone. Look near the fountain, that's where we'll be, with our squiggly tails, we swim in the sea! Can you find me?" You've got rhymes, a treasure hunt and culture rolled into one. Another guide, "Small Wonders" points out the tinier objects in the collection often overlooked.

Your kids will love spotting objects before you do. The Gardner has a series called "Family Fun Programs" held a few times a year on Saturday mornings. It is for children ages six though 10 accompanied by an adult. The cost is $20 a pair and after exploring the galleries you go to the art studio to try your hand at whatever the focus is that day, for example, drawing or sculpting. The museum also has a café with great food.

Museum of Fine Arts

465 Huntington Avenue
617-267-9300, www.mfa.org
Open daily, 10am-4:45pm, open until 9:45pm Wed.-Fri. (Only the West Wing is open late Thurs. and Fri. Tickets are $2 less after 5pm).
Closed Thanksgiving and Christmas.
Admission: $15, adults; children 7-17, $6.50 until 3pm (after 3pm, free); under 7, free. Your ticket allows you to visit twice in a 30-day period. After 4pm on Wednesday, admission is by voluntary contribution.
Take the Green Line to the Museum of Fine Arts stop. It's across the street.

The Museum of Fine Arts (MFA) is huge and can be intimidating to the uninitiated, or the very small. Rather than aimlessly dragging your kids around in an effort to find something that interests them, come on the weekend and stop by the Family Place (open Sat. and Sun., Oct.-June, 10am-4pm). You can begin the visit by playing games or working on puzzles. Museum instructors help you get going with suggestions and interesting facts. Activity books (always available at the Info Center) have self-guided tours. Depending on your child, you might decide to pick up "Fabulous Beasts West to East" or "Unravel the Mystery of the Mummy."

If you decide to head off on your own, it's a good idea to have a game plan in mind first. Pick two or three exhibits you want to visit, then call it quits. Nobody likes a cranky kid in a museum. The Egyptian Gallery is a no-brainer; kids always like the mummies. The Modern Art Gallery can make for interesting discussions. The Art of Africa Gallery fascinates children with beautiful masks.

There are three different food venues – an upscale restaurant with upscale prices, a café and a cafeteria. Those with kids will probably want to stick to the cafeteria downstairs.

Take 10

There aren't any close playgrounds in this area. Your best bet is heading to the Back Bay Fens and strolling along. There is plenty of green space for the kids to roam around.

The North End

The North End is the city's Italian section and you'll have no doubt about where you are while there. There is a real European feel to the area and food is a huge part of the neighborhood. You'll be tripping over bakeries and restaurants as you wander around the narrow streets. Every weekend in the summer saints are celebrated with processions and festivals, and lots of delicious, garlicky food. Since two of the Freedom Trail sites are located here (Paul Revere's House and the Old North Church), see if you can time your walk to coincide with lunch or dinnertime. Close your eyes, spin around and point. Eat there. You can't go wrong at any of the restaurants here.

Copp's Hill Burial Ground
Hull Street
Open daily, 9am-5pm (in the winter until 3pm); free.
Take the Orange or Green Line to Haymarket Station. Walk under the expressway to Cross Street. Follow the red painted Freedom Trail line to Salem Street.
Freedom Trail Site #14

The second-oldest burial ground in Boston is Copp's Hill, formerly called Windmill Hill. William Copp was a shoemaker who owned the land at one point. Many of the North End's artisans and merchants were buried here, along with free black people who lived in what was called the "New Guinea

Community." Robert Newman, the Old North Church sexton who warned Paul Revere that the British were coming, is also buried here. The British took aim from here at Charlestown during the Battle of Bunker Hill (that we all know was really Breed's Hill).

FleetCenter
Causeway Street
617-787-7678, www.fleetcenter.com
Take the Orange or Green Line to North Station.

Although the FleetCenter opened in 1995, it still is considered new in these parts. The FleetCenter has much to offer, such as comfort and visibility, two things that I like when parked somewhere for a couple of hours. The Boston Bruins and the Boston Celtics both call the FleetCenter home, but many other events happen here year-round. The circus, ice shows, concerts and more are just part of the schedule. The 2001 U.S. Figure Skating Championships were held here as were the first and second rounds of the 2003 NCAA Men's Basketball Tournament. In addition, the Sports Museum of New England is located on the fifth and sixth floors of the complex. (Details on the museum later.)

Old North Church
193 Salem Street
800-981-4776; 617-523-4848, www.oldnorth.com
Open daily June-October, 9am-6pm; November-May, 9am-5pm
Basic tour free, donations welcome; Behind the Scenes Tour in June-October is $8 for adults; $5 for children under 16. "Paul Revere Tonight" tickets are $12 for adults; $8, under 12. Summer shows. Call for times.
Take the Orange or Green Line to Haymarket.
Freedom Trail Site #13

Two lanterns swinging from the belfry in the Old North Church set in motion Paul Revere's famous ride setting off the

Revolutionary War. The sexton of the church, Robert Newman (who is buried in Copp's Hill), hung the lanterns on April 18, 1775, to warn that the British were coming up the Charles River en route to Lexington. The Old Church is still open for services and welcomes visitors. It was built in 1723 and is quite beautiful. In addition to its Paul Revere fame, the church is home to the oldest church bells in North America. The Old North Church's gardens are a wonderful spot to rest if you are walking the Freedom Trail. Children might enjoy the "Paul Revere Tonight" show, where a costumed actor recounts this famous citizen's early years in Boston.

Paul Revere House

19 North Square
617-523-2338, www.paulreverehouse.org
Open: Mid-April-October 9:30am-5:15pm; Nov.-April 14, 9:30am-4:15pm; closed Mondays January-March.
Admission: Adults, $3; children 5-17, $1.
Take the Green or Orange Line T to Haymarket Station.
Freedom Trail Site #12

Paul Revere owned the house from 1770 through 1800 and this is where he took off from for his famous ride. The house is the oldest remaining building in the downtown area. It was built around 1680 and much of the original building is intact.

I recommend scheduling a visit to coincide with one of the many events held throughout the year at the museum. On Saturdays, May through October, programs about life in colonial Boston are fascinating to children. Everything from music to cutting silhouettes is demonstrated. Occasionally actors portray Revere and his wife, his mother-in-law and many others, and answer questions about their roles during the Revolutionary War. Going to one of these programs is probably more engaging to children than a mere tour around the museum.

Sports Museum of New England
On the 5th & 6th floors of the FleetCenter
Causeway Street
617-624-1235, www.sportsmuseum.org
Open: Schedule depends on FleetCenter events. Always call before going.
Generally open Monday-Saturday, 11am-5pm and Sunday 11am-3pm.
Admission is granted on the hour until 3pm (last entry).
Admission: Adults, $6; children 6-17, $4; under 6, free. Buy your tickets at the
FleetCenter box office.
Take the Orange or Green Line to North Station.

For the sports fans in the family, this is an essential stop. Exhibits cover the gamut – boxing, hockey, football, basketball, soccer and baseball. Pretend you're catching a fastball from Roger Clemens at one interactive exhibit, watch old footage of the Boston Garden (true fans still lament its demise, but you can sit in old Garden seats at least!), and learn about local high school and college teams. Don't miss the Boston Bruins Hall of Fame portraits or the exhibit on the Boston Marathon.

Take 10 – Langone Park
Commercial Street

This sweet little playground has got one of the best views in town and everything you need for relaxing after wandering around the North End. It even has a public bathroom, a nice clean one, modeled after those in Paris. You'll have to pay a quarter to use it, but I've had to spend a lot more at various restaurants or coffee shops to gain access to the toilet. Anyway, the playground sits right on the edge (almost) of the Charles River. It's enclosed, has swings and a climbing structure and a nearby spray fountain at the Mirabella Pool next door is great in hot weather.

Charlestown

Ten Puritan families settled Charlestown in 1629 and it remained its own community until 1874, when it was annexed to Boston. The Battle of Bunker Hill (aka Breed's Hill) occurred here in 1775, which you can learn about at the monument. The town was pretty much destroyed by the famous battle and then rebuilt after the American Revolution. The Charlestown Navy Yard, no longer in operation, is a national historic monument and home to the USS *Constitution*. Tours of the ship and the nearby museum offer a fascinating look into its glorious past.

Bunker Hill Monument
55 Constitution Road
Charlestown, MA 02129
617-241-7575
Open daily, 9am-4:30pm
Free
Take the Orange or Green Line T to North Station. Walk down Causeway Street to N. Washington Street. Turn left, cross the Charlestown Bridge. Follow the Freedom Trail line.
Freedom Trail Site #16

The first major battle of the Revolutionary War took place on Breed's Hill, so we have a monument on Bunker Hill. Also, we actually lost this battle but we have a monument anyway. Breed's Hill was a better vantage point than the higher up Bunker Hill for the colonists to try to repel the British. They managed to fight off two waves of attacks from the British, killing half of them, before retreating. Although losing the battle, this proved the colonists could really fight and gave them hope for future battles.

You can climb up the 221-foot-high monument to get great views of the city. Little kids won't be able to make this trek. Go to the Bunker Hill Pavilion to see more on the battle in a movie called "Whites of Their Eyes." The name of the movie comes from the legend that the colonists weren't supposed to fire until they saw the whites of the Redcoats' eyes.

Bunker H ill © *Greater Boston Visitors & Convention Bureau*

Kim Foley MacKinnon

Charlestown Navy Yard
National Historical Park
Charlestown, MA 02129
617-242-5601; free.
Take the Orange or Green Line T to North Station. Walk down Causeway
Street to N. Washington Street. Turn left, cross the Charlestown Bridge.
Follow the Freedom Trail line.

The Charlestown Navy Yard, now part of the park system, was
once a thriving shipyard, used for 174 years. It was one of the
first shipyards built in the United States but before that, the
British used the spot to land on before the Battle of Bunker Hill.
You can walk around and see what remains of the shipyard, but
the biggest draw here is the USS *Constitution*.

USS *Constitution* and Museum
Charlestown Navy Yard
Box 1812
Boston, MA 02129
617-426-1812
www.ussconstitutionnavy.mil; www.ussconstitutionmuseum.org
Ship: Tours given Thursday-Sunday, noon-4pm.
Museum: Open May-November, 9am-6pm; November-April, 10am-5pm.
Both are free. See above for directions.
Freedom Trail Site #15

"Old Ironsides," as the oldest commissioned warship afloat is
affectionately called, makes its home at the Charlestown Navy
Yard. If you ever get a chance to see the ship out in the harbor,
it's a sight you'll never forget. Crewmembers give tours of the
vessel, which was built in 1797. The *Constitution* is most
renowned for fighting off five British ships in the War of 1812.
Visit the nearby museum for exhibits, hands-on activities and
artifacts detailing the long history of the warship.

Take 10 – Paul Revere Park

The Paul Revere Park on Constitution Road in Charlestown is a fabulous place to make a stop after visiting the USS *Constitution* and Bunker Hill, especially if you climbed up the monument! There are five acres to roam around and have a picnic; a fenced-in playground; and a great view of the Charles River.

"Old Ironsides" © *Greater Boston Visitors & Convention Bureau*

Kim Foley MacKinnon

Jamaica Plain, Roslindale, Roxbury & Dorchester

These neighborhoods, once home to the richest Bostonians, are part of the city, but often get a bad rap or are ignored altogether. Although their fortunes fell, they are on the rise again. There are some sights definitely worth seeking out in these areas. Jamaica Plain, or "JP" to those who live there, is the latest urban renewal success story. The area prides itself on its diversity. The main drag, Centre Street, is packed with every type of cuisine, from Thai to Latino to Indian. Jamaica Pond is a serene setting in the thriving neighborhood. Roslindale is hard on Jamaica Plain's heels and shares the Arnold Arboretum with it. The Franklin Park Zoo in Roxbury is one of those jewels in the Emerald Necklace. In Dorchester, two popular sites to visit are the JFK Library & Museum, and the city's major paper, *The Boston Globe*.

Arnold Arboretum
125 Arborway
Jamaica Plain/Roslindale
617-524-1718, www.arboretum.harvard.edu
Open dawn to dusk daily. Free.
Take the Orange Line T to Forest Hills.

Come here and forget that you are in Boston. More than 250 acres of open space makes this easy to do. You can bike, in-line skate, run or just stroll among the walkways in this beautiful park, yet another Boston jewel in Frederick Law Olmsted's Emerald Necklace. The only thing you can't do here is picnic, tempting as it may be. Oh, you can't pick anything or climb anything either – the Arboretum is a National Historic Landmark and part of Harvard University. This is a wonderful place for city dwellers to bring their kids to learn how to ride their bikes or to

54

show them there is more to the world than sidewalks and stoplights. Lilac Sunday (on Mother's Day) in May is the one exception to the no-picnicking rule and brings crowds of people happy to celebrate the spring and flowers.

Bay State Society of Model Engineers Museum
760 South St.
Roslindale
617-327-4341
Open Wednesdays from noon to 6pm by appointment.
Take the Orange Line to Forest Hill and then a bus to Roslindale Village. Or take the commuter rail to the Roslindale Village stop.

This is a very unique museum located in Roslindale. This former private club-turned museum has three prominent scale model trains: O-, HO-, and N-gauge. Most clubs focus on one size or maybe two, not all three.

Most of the scenes recreated in miniature in the huge second-floor space are from the 1930's through the 1950's. A visitor can view the mining towns of Colorado to the plains of Iowa by crossing the room. A replica 1940's Roslindale Square, complete with the society's building, is currently under construction.

Besides historically accurate trains, period automobiles are also made by members. Calling it "kit bashing," the engineers often add elements to model kit trains and cars because they aren't authentic enough. Such details include painstakingly adding chrome to train window frames or painting car seats the color the originals left the factory with. For train buffs, this is a must.

The Boston Globe
135 Morrissey Boulevard
Dorchester, MA 02107
617-929-2653
Tours given Monday & Thursday, 10am, 11:15am & 1:15pm, by appointment only. Also one Wednesday night a month.
Free
Children must be over 9 years old.
Take the Red Line to the JFK/UMASS stop. Walk down Morrissey Boulevard.

For a behind-the-scenes look at Boston's major paper, the Boston Globe, you'll have to plan in advance. You get to see the newsroom (and you thought the kids' rooms were messy!), composing room and press room. Children might be surprised at how putting together a paper really works.

Boston Nature Center
500 Walk Hill Street
Mattapan, MA 02126 (near Roslindale & Jamaica Plain)
617-983-8500, www.massaudubon.org
Nature Center: Monday-Friday, 9am-5pm; Saturday, Sunday, and Monday holidays, 10am-4pm.
Trails: Open every day, dawn to dusk.
Suggested Donation, $2 for nonmembers
Boston Nature Center is bounded by Morton Street (Route 203), American Legion Highway, Walk Hill Street and Harvard Street.

You'll find two miles of trails and boardwalks that meander through meadows and wetlands. Wildlife includes coyotes, pheasants and many species of migratory birds. The sanctuary's George Robert White Environmental Conservation Center is one of the "greenest" buildings in Boston, teaching environmentally sustainable design by example. The Clark-Cooper Community Gardens located here are Boston's oldest and largest community gardens, with 260 families using it. Classes and lectures are offered.

Forest Hills Cemetery
95 Forest Hills Avenue
Jamaica Plain
617-524-0128; www.foresthillstrust.org
Open 8:30am until dusk
Take the Orange Line to the Forest Hills stop.

Most people don't think of cemeteries exactly as the perfect spot to take children, but you shouldn't dismiss them out of hand.

A little background is in order. Forest Hills was founded in 1848 by Henry Dearborn, then the mayor of Roxbury. Through its 150- year history, it has grown into 275 acres of green space. There are numerous species of plants and trees from around the world on site, and countless beautiful sculptures can be found here. People come to take walks, have picnics and yes, let their kids roam (as well as their dogs).

Exhibits are often staged here and there are a number of guided or self-guided tours you can take.

Franklin Park Zoo
One Franklin Park Road
617-541-LION
www.zoonewengland.com
Open: April-September, 10am-5pm, weekends until 6 pm.
October-March, daily 10am-4pm.
Admission: Adults, $8.50; children 2-15, $4; under 2, free.
Take the Orange Line to Forest Hills, then catch the number 16 bus. If you are driving, this is one of the few places around Boston that has free, plentiful parking.

The Franklin Park Zoo sits in the 500-acre Franklin Park, part of the Emerald Necklace. Around the zoo, don't be surprised to see golfers zipping around in golf carts. There is an 18-hole course in the park as well as a pond and a 100-acre woods (not the

Hundred Acre Woods, alas). The 72-acre zoo has gotten a facelift in recent years, making it a much better place to visit. More than 20 new exhibits have been installed here and at its sister zoo, the Stone Zoo in Stoneham.

The Franklin Farm exhibit allows children to pet cows and goats and also always get a thumbs-up. The Butterfly Landing, open only in the summer, has more than 1,000 butterflies to gaze at in wonder (it's an extra $1 for this exhibit). All the other usual suspects can be found as well – lions, kangaroos, and giraffes. The zoo covers a lot of ground so a stroller or backpack is a good idea.

Jamaica Pond & Boathouse
The Jamaicaway
617-522-6258 (boathouse), 617-522-4573 (rangers)
www.jamaicaplain.com
Boat rentals: rowboat $8 Boston residents/$10 nonresidents per hour – sailboat $15/$20.
Take the Riverway south from Route 9.

Few neighborhood parks are so well used and well loved as Jamaica Pond, and for good reason. The grounds are well maintained, the vibe is relaxed and friendly, and glimpses of nature are everywhere to be enjoyed, right in the middle of a city neighborhood. It also happens to be the site of America's first reservoir and part of the Emerald Necklace. In every season and at just about any daylight hour, the pond's paved trail is occupied by people of all ages and from many walks of life. It's a place to kick back and enjoy the small pleasures of childhood: feeding the ducks and geese; tossing sticks and rocks; spotting a majestic swan, a shy turtle, numerous dogs; walking, running and riding; having a picnic and meeting old or new friends. (Adults are not allowed to use bikes or in-line skates, except on the outer trail close to the road. Younger children can skate or ride by the pond's bank as long as they are supervised.) Children under five will enjoy just being there. Older kids will be more interested in sledding on the very steep hill just adjacent to the pond or getting out on the water in a rented boat.

You can rent sailboats July through Labor Day; rowboats, April through September. Call ahead because weekends are busy. Jamaica Pond also hosts a number of festive but low-key seasonal celebrations. One of the best, (but maybe a little scary for small children), is the Lantern Parade. This is held every year when we push back the clocks. Nothing is more beautiful than seeing hundreds of homemade lanterns glowing in the night as people make their way around the pond.

John F. Kennedy Library and Museum
Columbia Point
Dorchester, MA 02125
877-616-4599
www.jfklibrary.org
Open daily 9am-5pm; closed Thanksgiving, Christmas & New Year's Day.
Admission: Adults, $8; 13-17, $4; under 12, free; special exhibits extra.
Take the Red Line T to JFK/UMass station; take a free shuttle bus to the library.

This is the place to learn everything you ever wanted to know about JFK. The museum has 25 exhibits detailing his life and presidency. Although much of the museum's content is targeted for adults and older children, most kids can enjoy the mock-up of certain White House rooms. There's the "White House Hall," with rooms off of it leading to the "Oval Office" and also a re-creation of his brother Robert F. Kennedy's Justice Department office. A piece of the Berlin Wall is also on display at the I.M. Pei-designed library. Jacqueline Kennedy is not neglected; many exhibits show off her interests. As you leave, you'll pass through an atrium, 115 feet high, where a gigantic American flag is displayed and which has fantastic views of Boston. The museum café is also a great place to enjoy the same views of the harbor.

Olmsted Park
Perkins Street
Take the Riverway south from Route 9.

This namesake park for the master planner of the Emerald Necklace, Frederick Law Olmsted, is composed of three ponds, numerous walkways with footbridges and a bike path. It is between the Jamaica Pond area and the Riverway, both jewels in the necklace. You could meander endlessly throughout the park system. Kids learning to ride their bikes can't ask for a better place to go. This is also a fabulous place to come with older kids to go sledding when it snows. The hills guarantee a wild ride.

Take 10
I can't give just one playground for this section because these areas are so wide apart. If you are near Dorchester, head over to Castle Island in South Boston. The zoo has a playground of its own in the unlikely event the kids should tire of the animals. It's right next to the snack bar area, which means you can watch them play while you finish eating. Over in JP, a wonderful Tot Lot for smaller children has more toys than you'll see at any other playground. Residents bring toys and leave them for others to use. The well-cared-for playground has climbing structures and a sand box. If you are at Jamaica Pond, cross the Jamaicaway (go to the crosswalk!) at Pond Street. Take a right on the parkway. Go one block to Burroughs Street. Go down one block to Brewer Street and you'll see it.

Greater Boston

Several of the following sites are located in Brookline, which is not a part of Boston, but is nestled right next to it. A large Jewish population makes their home here, which is evident in the many delis and kosher restaurants up and down Harvard Square (where else are you going to find a kosher Chinese restaurant?). The Green Line "C" train will drop you off at Coolidge Corner, the main part of the town. The Larz Anderson Park is a great spot for families. South Boston, or "Southie," often ignored in many guidebooks, does have some charming areas, too. Carson Beach and Castle Island are a lot of fun in the summer. The closest place to do real hiking or cross-country skiing is in Milton, at the Blue Hills Reservation. You have 7,000 acres to lose yourself in exploring.

Allandale Farm
259 Allandale Road
Brookline, MA 02467
617-524-1531
www.allandalefarm.com
Open: April-December, 10am-6pm
Free
Directions: You have to have a car for this one. From Boston, take Route 1 South to the Jamaicaway. Follow the signs for Faulkner Hospital, Dedham and West Roxbury. Turn right at the hospital on Allandale Road.

The last working farm in Boston and Brookline is Allandale Farm, which raises organic fruits and vegetables. At their store, you can buy all sorts of seasonal products from Christmas trees to watermelons. Hayrides in October are fun for kids and you can sign up for a workshop on making scarecrows. A unique summer camp program is held here from mid-June through mid-August for children ages 4-10. The three-hour morning camp introduces children to gardening, identifying birds and plants, animals and more. Annually, outdoor sculptures make an appearance at the farm during the Brookline Artists' Open Studios event each spring. This is definitely a great place to show city kids that vegetables don't grow in the grocery store.

Blue Hills Trailside Museum & Reservation

1904 Canton Avenue
Milton, MA 02186
617-333-0690, www.massaudubon.org
Trails open: Daily dawn to dusk, all year. Museum: Tuesday-Sunday, 10am-5pm.
Admission: Adults, $3; children 3-12, $1.50. Mass Audubon members, free.
Take Rte. 128 (93) from Boston to exit 2B (Milton) to Rte. 138 North. It's a half-mile on the right.

There is enough to do at the almost 7,000-acre reservation to qualify it as a day-trip destination. There are 150 miles of trails to explore, plus the museum, which has exhibits detailing the wildlife you might encounter while hiking around. In my book, however, what is great here are all the various programs offered throughout the year. On weekends, there is story time at 11am (for ages 3-6), plus the "mystery species" presentation at 1pm (for all ages). At 3pm, the "theme of the month" is explored (ages 6 and up). The theme might be "Animal Coverings," "Tracking" or "Bones and Skulls." These are all free with general admission. Other special programs such as "Owl Hootenany" and "Maple Sugar Days" are a blast. You can see owls up close and collect sap in buckets. These programs are extra, but completely worth it. Check out the Mass. Audubon Society's website for other events.

Carson Beach
Day Boulevard
South Boston, MA 02127
Take the Red Line to the JFK/UMass stop. It's a two minute walk. Or driving: from Boston, take Route 3 to the JFK Exit, follow the beach along Day Boulevard.

You don't have to leave the city to go to the beach. Carson Beach, located near Castle Island, offers swimming, with lifeguards in the summer and really fabulous views. You're not going to mistake it for Cape Cod or anything, but the kids won't care. Sand castles and poking around with sticks is fun on any beach. On a hot, sticky city day, heading down here to cool off can't be beat.

Castle Island
Day Boulevard
South Boston, MA 02127
617-268-5744
Open year-round; tours of the fort on summer weekends only
From Boston, take Route 3 to the JFK Exit, follow the beach along Day Boulevard until the end.

First off, don't look for a castle and you're not on an island. Castle Island is just one more place in Boston that does not seem to be named correctly, although to be fair it was once an island, in the 1600s. What is here is Fort Independence, which was built between 1834 and 1851. It doesn't matter what it's called though, this is a great place to have a picnic, Rollerblade, swim, watch the planes fly in and out of Logan, and look out at the harbor. There is also a great Tot Lot for the kids to play. A snack bar offers French fries and frappes. You can also fish from the pier.

Kidport at Logan Airport
Terminal C, Logan Airport
617-561-1600, www.massport.com
Take the Blue Line T the airport. Take a free shuttle bus to Terminal C.

Maybe this sounds like a strange destination. After all, who wants to go to the airport if they can help it? But, hey, if you're already there, this is a lifesaver. And if you don't have to hop a plane, but need an activity sure to please, this is a fun outing for kids, even tiny ones. There's an infant area plus lots of fun stuff to climb on for the bigger kids.

Larz Anderson Park
Bounded by Newton Street, Avon Street and Goddard Avenue
Brookline, MA 02146
617-730-2069, www.townofbrooklinemass.com
Ice-skating: December-February. Adults, $7, children, $4 (skate rental extra).
Hours open: Friday, 7:30pm-9:30pm; Saturday, noon-5pm & 7:30-9:30pm;
Sunday, noon-5pm.

Larz Anderson Park, with 64 acres, has everything one could hope for in a park: an excellent playground, a picnic table area, barbecue pits, a pond, and an outdoor ice-skating rink and sports fields. Don't miss the Temple of Love pavilion sitting on the edge of the lagoon. It's a pleasant spot to sit. The views of Boston are amazing. In the summer, you can have a fabulous cookout or picnic if you reserve in advance. Come winter, strap on skates and take a whirl on the ice.

This park is more a resident pleasure since it is not really accessible by the T. If you are a major car buff, you can visit the Museum of Transportation (see below) and then let the kids run around in the enclosed playground here afterwards.

Museum of Transportation

15 Newton Street, Larz Anderson Park
Brookline, MA 02146
617-522-6140, www.mot.org
Open: Tuesday-Sunday, 10am-5pm and Monday holidays.
Admission: Adults, $5; children, 6-18, $3; under 6, free.
See above directions to Larz Anderson Park.

The centerpiece of the Larz Anderson Park in Brookline is the Museum of Transportation. The core of the museum is the original stable of early automobiles donated to the city of Boston as part of the Larz Anderson estate and housed in the original carriage house. While the rotating exhibits upstairs are strictly off-limits to little fingers, the downstairs is devoted exclusively to tiny car lovers, and other than a large collection of vintage and rare automobile toys, allows for interaction. There is a pedal kart ride-on carousel, the bridge of a Boston Trolley with bell, continuously running, automobile-related "Little Rascals" episodes and coloring supplies on a crafts table. Through spring, summer and fall there are also weekly Sunday lawn events with marquee theme days free with museum admission.

"Beep!" © *Elizabeth Seitz*

Cambridge & Harvard Square

One nickname for Cambridge you might hear bandied about is "Boston's Left Bank." Another is "The People's Republic of Cambridge." This is due to its liberal leanings and independent character from Boston. Harvard University and the Massachusetts Institute of Technology are the big names around here. Each square in Cambridge – Harvard, Central, Inman, Kendall and Porter – has its own charms. If you are new to the city, you'll probably head for Harvard Square first. Since this is more a guidebook for the other side of the Charles River, I've touched only on a few favorites, most of them around Harvard Square. Cambridge has much to offer.

Harvard Square is a destination by itself, offering endless people watching and entertainment, all for free. Any warm night brings out crowds of people, all happy to just hang out. Any number of musicians and performers come out too, which make the square an exciting spot to be. There are so many bookstores in Harvard Square that the tourist board puts out a bookstore guide to help tourists find all 24 of them. In recent years, the individual character of the square has been lost a little as big-name stores have moved in, pushing out independents. I guess that's the price of progress. But the spirit of the area hasn't been diminished. Any visit to Harvard Square is not complete without wandering around the Harvard University campus, the oldest university in the United States.

Curious George Goes to Wordsworth
1 JFK Street, Harvard Square
Cambridge, MA 02138
617-498-0062
Open Mon.-Sat., 9am-9pm, Sun., 10am-8pm
Take the Red Line T to Harvard Square.

Right in the heart of Harvard Square is a store begging for your attention. The bright yellow storefront will surely catch yours and your children's eyes as you wander about. Oh, that familiar monkey won't be lost on your kids either. Wordsworth, a wonderful independent bookstore down the block, is the parent of this charming store. Two floors are packed with books and toys that are not to be found at every bookstore. Of course, Curious George books and paraphernalia are everywhere, but by no means is that all. Try to get out of here without buying something. I have yet to do so.

Harvard Museum of Natural History
26 Oxford Street
Cambridge, MA 02138
617-495-3045, www.hmnh.harvard.edu
Open daily 9am-5pm. Closed New Year's Day, Thanksgiving and Christmas.
Admission: Adults, $7; children, $5; under 3, free.
Free on Wednesdays, 3-5pm, and Sundays, 9am-noon.
Take the Red line to Harvard Square. The Museum is located through Harvard Yard. Cross through the Yard and go up Oxford Street. It's the fourth building on the right.

This is one of Boston's hidden treasures. I don't know of many locals who have been here, which is too bad because they are missing out on a unique museum. Located in one rather sprawling structure, the Harvard Museum of Natural History shares the building with the Botanical Museum, the Museum of Comparative Zoology and the Mineralogical and Geological Museum (admission covers all, plus the Peabody Museum of Archaeology and Ethnology – not always a big kid hit, so it's safe to skip it). Sheer numbers are what get you here: 3,000 glass flowers, a 1,642-pound amethyst, a 42-foot-long prehistoric marine reptile, and so on. The vast amount of taxidermy animals (we call them "statues" for our young animal lover) is unbelievable. It seems that the energetic Harvard ancestors caught one of every creature in the world and displayed it here. They are so lifelike, you might jump when you see the tiger! You'll have to drag the kids away from here.

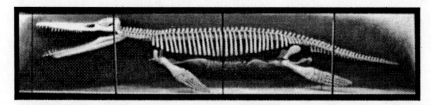

Kronosaurus from the Harvard Museum of Natural History
Charles Mayer © President and Fellows of Harvard College

Harvard University
26 Oxford Street
Cambridge, MA 02138
617-495-1573
www.harvard.edu
Free tours: Offered during the academic year. Call for times.
Take the Red Line T to the Harvard Square stop.

Although you can walk through Harvard Yard any time, I recommend going on a tour if you can. The student guides are full of information about the history and architecture of the nation's first university (founded in 1636), and tell you all about the libraries and museums on campus. They describe the life of a Harvard student and make the place seem a little less intimidating. Funny stories and lore make the tour a little more interesting for older kids. Little ones will probably enjoy people watching and being pushed or carried around as you explore. There are plenty of places to just sit and relax in the shade of a 200-year-old tree. Look for the statue of John Harvard, which makes for a good story. The statue, sculpted in 1884, is just an idea of what the artist thought he looked like, as there are no known images of Harvard. Also, the school was founded in 1636, not 1638 and, finally, Harvard was not the founder, he was a benefactor.

If you're not around for a tour, walk around. The university is quite beautiful and surprisingly quiet and peaceful. Don't forget to tell the kids that six U.S. presidents attended Harvard. Maybe they'll get inspired.

Minuteman Bikeway
Runs from Alewife Station in Cambridge to Lexington.
For a map, visit www.state.ma.us and click on maps, then click bicycle maps.

For the biking family, this is a great and very popular bike path that was once a railroad corridor. It closely follows the path that Paul Revere took on his way to Lexington. Of course, maybe riding with your kids in back or alongside you for 10 miles or so is not your idea of fun. Nobody said you had to do the whole thing!

There are many places to take breaks, and signs point out nearby restaurants and facilities. The bikeway can get a little crowded, though. Remind the kids to stay on the right side of the path and look out for faster bikers. It's a nice, well-maintained path that makes it easy for kids to ride.

MIT Museum
265 Massachusetts Avenue
Cambridge, MA 02139
617-253-4444, www.web.mit.edu/museum
Open: Tuesday-Friday, 10am-5pm; Sat. & Sun., noon-5pm.
Cost: Adults, $5; children 5-18, $2. Third Sunday of the month, free.
Take the Red Line T to the Central Square stop.

The Massachusetts Institute of Technology's museum has the world's largest collection of holography. If your kids have ever gotten any hologram cards out of cereal boxes and thought they were cool, wait until they see them here. Holograms are really the tip of the iceberg at this interactive museum, which has all sorts of cutting-edge technology displays. Hands-on is the order of the day here, where kids can watch what the heat of their hands does to the plasma globes. Kids also might like the "Hall of Hacks," where notorious pranks by MIT students are displayed, although you probably don't want to encourage your kids in this direction!

MIT also offers family programs. New themes are introduced each month at the Invention Studio. You might use Twinkies in the "Gastobot" series or use an Etch-a-Sketch in a "Art on the Screen" program. The cost is $25 per adult/child team. Also, on the last Sunday of the month during the school year, from 2-4pm, come in for a free (with admission) program on science given by staff and students. You'll work on a project related to something going on at the school. Prove to your kids that science can be fun!

To learn more about MIT itself, take a tour of the campus. Like Harvard, students give the tours and love to tell anecdotes. Call 617-253-4795. The museum gift shop is another great place to pick up unusual gifts and souvenirs.

Mount Auburn Cemetery
580 Mt. Auburn Street
Cambridge, MA 02138
617-547-7105, www.mountauburn.com
Take the Red Line T to Harvard Square.

This attractive 174-acre cemetery makes for a beautiful and peaceful walk, even with kids in tow. It was the first garden cemetery in the US and was landscaped as an arboretum. Henry Wadsworth Longfellow and other notables are buried here. From the tower on the grounds you have a 360-degree view of the surrounding area. Pick up a walking-tour pamphlet at the gatehouse that has a map of famous graves as well as descriptions of flora and fauna. You can take in a little history while the kids stretch their legs.

Take 10 – Cambridge Common

At the meeting of Massachusetts Avenue and Garden Street your kids can play where the Continental Army once trained. The large playground, complete with swings and tons of structures to climb on, is a couple of blocks from Harvard Square, but well worth seeking out. There is a picnic table and the playground is enclosed. Look for the Civil War monument and one about the Irish famine.

Three:
The Freedom Trail & Beyond

Follow the Leader

Boston has a trail or a tour for just about everything. From a historical perspective of colonial America to even more specialized tours, such as literary, women's history, black heritage, or a hunt for the solar system here on earth, you should be able to find one to interest the whole family. Some of the trails are probably too long for smaller kids so just be creative and tailor the walks to suit your family. Older children might be able to connect a trail and its sights to a school project. You can also make it fun for the kids if you pose it as a treasure hunt. Arranged tours on a bus or a duck boat (more on that later!) are wonderful if walking is not your thing. Hopping on and off a bus may appeal to you for the chance to rest in between sightseeing and let someone else tell you about the sites. Many of the individual sights on the trails are listed under their specific area of Boston in the previous chapter.

The Freedom Trail

This is the most famous of all the Boston trails. Follow the red painted line, about 2.5 miles long, for a tour of 16 sites from the Colonial and Revolutionary era. Most sites are free but a few do charge admission. Start off at the Boston Common Visitor Information Center, near the Park Street T stop, where you can pick up a copy of the trail sites and any other information you might need. To properly see everything, you'll need more than a day. Pick and choose what is most important to your family and skip the rest. Visit www.thefreedomtrail.org. for a virtual tour.

Shorter tours are given by the National Park Service (617-242-5642; www.nps.gov) April-November, which visit most, but not all, of the sites. They also have a few additional sites, which differ from the Freedom Trail. Tours start at the Boston National Historic Park Visitor Center across from the Old State House.

1. Boston Common: The Common is bordered by Tremont, Boylston and Beacon streets. Once a cattle grazing field, it's now a public park smack dab in the middle of the city.
2. Massachusetts State House: Beacon Street. The beautiful gold-domed State House is the oldest building on Beacon Hill.
3. Park Street Church: One Park St. Founded in 1809.
4. Granary Burying Ground: Tremont St., next to the Park Street Church. Samuel Adams, Paul Revere and John Hancock are buried here.
5. King's Chapel & Burying Ground: Corner of Tremont and School streets. Nobody would sell the British governor land to build a non-Puritan church in 1688, so he built one on the town burying ground. So there.
6. Site of the First Public School & Ben Franklin Statue: School St. The school (Boston Latin) has since moved but a plaque and Franklin show where the country's first public school once stood.
7. Old Corner Bookstore: One School Street. Literary gathering place and publishing house.
8. Old South Meeting House: 310 Washington Street. A meeting here in 1773 set off that famous Boston Tea Party.
9. Old State House: Corner of State and Washington streets. The Declaration of Independence was first read from the Old State House balcony of the oldest surviving public building in Boston.

10. Boston Massacre Site: Next to the Old State House. Look for the ring of cobblestones on a traffic island where this incident occurred.

11. Faneuil Hall: Merchants Row. Many meetings in this 250-year-old hall led to changes in the course of history.

12. Paul Revere House: 19 North Square.

13. Old North Church: 193 Salem Street. The two lanterns signaling the British were coming were hung from this church's steeple in 1775.

14. Copp's Hill Burial Ground: Uphill from the Old North Church. Sexton Robert Newman, who hung the famous lanterns in the Old North Church, is buried here,

15. USS *Constitution*: Pier 1, Charlestown. Also know as "Old Ironsides;" it is the oldest commissioned warship afloat.

16. Bunker Hill Monument: Monument Square, Charlestown. A monument marking the site of first major battle of the American Revolution.

Community Solar System Hunt

This is great fun and can give your kids a sense of scale in the big scheme of things. It's a treasure hunt of the solar system, sponsored by the Museum of Science as part of its "Welcome to the Universe" exhibit. The "Sun" is located at the museum and the planets are placed at accurate proportions throughout the city. The scale is 400 million to 1! An inch equals 6,215 miles.

To start off, get a "Community Solar System Passport," either online at www.mos.org or at the museum. Track down the planets and do a pencil rubbing of the planet's symbol found on the sculpture on the correct page of the passport. When finished, send it to the museum and they'll send you a certificate of completion. The passport has directions to each of the "planets" as well as fun facts. They can all be reached by public transportation, but be warned, a couple are out of the city.

1. Sun: In the Museum of Science "Welcome to the Universe" exhibit.

2. Mercury: In the Museum of Science, in the front plaza.

3. Venus: In the Museum of Science, on the roof of the garage near the Gilliland Observatory.

4. Earth: Royal Sonesta Hotel, on the brick walkway in the courtyard.

5. Mars: Cambridgeside Galleria Mall, 2nd floor balcony, in front of elevators.

6. Jupiter: South Station, in the Grand Concourse near the Food Court.

7. Saturn: Cambridge Public Library, in the Anthony J. DeVito Music Room.

8. Uranus: Jamaica Plain Branch of the Boston Public Library, in the entryway, near periodicals.

9. Neptune: Square One Mall, Saugus, in the Food Court.

10. Pluto: Riverside Station, Newton, on the train platform.

Mail your passport to: Community Solar System, Charles Hayden Planetarium, Science Park, Boston, MA, 02114. Call 617-723-2500 or visit www.mos.org. if you need more info.

Big Dig Tour or "The CA/T Walk"
Massachusetts Turnpike Authority
Central Artery/Tunnel Authority
185 Kneeland Street
Boston, MA 02111
617-951-6400, www.bigdig.com

This self-guided walking tour of the Big Dig is provided by the Massachusetts Turnpike Authority. As this is an evolving project, I highly recommend calling or checking on the website before visiting. Things change all the time. You can get a walking tour map booklet with more details sent to you via e-mail or faxed to you. If you don't feel like doing the whole tour, take a look at the seven sites below anyway. You might be nearby a site while en route to somewhere else. The Big Dig truly is an amazing project.

Here is the tour as it stands now. I have given detailed directions since you need to be looking from specific sites to see the work in progress. No hardhat needed.

1. South Station Bus Terminal: Take the Red Line to South Station. Follow signs to the bus terminal. Look out from the glass-enclosed staircase on the second floor of the terminal. Workers are building 2,000 feet of a new underground highway. This is part of the Big Dig's largest tunnel construction.

2. A Street/Mt. Washington Avenue: From the bus terminal, head back to the South Station Commuter Rail and Amtrak platforms. Enter the concourse area and exit through Summer Street doors. Go down Summer Street, cross the Fort Point Channel on the Summer Street Bridge and take your first right on Melcher St. Follow to the end and take a right on A Street. Stay on the pedestrian walkway. After you pass a tall sound barrier wall take a right on Mt. Washington Avenue. Here you'll see a construction area where crews are building an eight-lane highway under the Fort Point Channel. This is a very tricky part of the project because of bad soil conditions and it's right next to the Red Line.

3. Summer Street/Congress Street Kiosk: Go back to A Street, following the pedestrian walkways to view the South Boston tunnel construction to the right of A Street. Then follow Summer Street to Congress Street where you can stop on the bridge at an info kiosk.

4. Dewey Square/Atlantic Avenue: Go back to South Station and pass by the front. Here are Plexiglas windows to look through at what will be the deepest point under Dewey Point, 120 feet below the Red Line. Cross Summer Street and go north on

Atlantic Avenue. You'll come to Vent Building #3, under construction between Congress St. and Northern Ave. The vent building will supply fresh air to the tunnels and remove exhaust.
5. Surface Artery: High Street to State Street. Continue down Atlantic Ave. to the Boston Harbor Hotel. Cross Atlantic Ave. onto Surface Artery. You are directly below the elevated highway. Underneath your feet construction is ongoing to build the underground highway.
6. Haymarket: Continue on Surface Artery north and take a left into Marketplace Center. Take a right in front of Quincy Market. Go straight to Clinton Street at the Dock Square Parking Garage. Follow Clinton to the end and take a right onto North Street. Follow signs to the North End. Take a left before the elevated artery. Go through the Haymarket vendors and look for the large Freedom Trail sign. Take the passageway under the Central Artery and you'll find more Plexiglas windows to check out the tunnel construction.
7. MDC Charles River Dam: Keep on the passageway and cross over Cross Street. Bear right on Endicott Street and then take a left on Stillman Place. Take a right on North Washington Street and go three blocks to the Causeway Street intersection. Cross Causeway St. and go left. Go right on Beverly Street and look for signs to Lovejoy Wharf. Pass the wharf and enter the MDC Charles River Dam pedestrian walkway. Follow until you get to the Paul Revere Landing Park in Charlestown, one of the new parks created during the project.

Black Heritage Trail
As the name states, this is a trail tracing the history of African Americans who settled in this area of Beacon Hill between 1800 and 1900. Like the Freedom Trail, it starts at Boston Common. Call the Boston African American National Historic Site for more info at 617-742-5415.

1. Robert Gould Shaw & 54th Regiment Memorial: At the entrance to Boston Common at Park and Beacon streets. Honors the service of African Americans in the Civil War. Shaw, who was white, volunteered to lead the first black regiment in the North.

2. George Middleton House: 5 Pinckney Street. Oldest home built by a black person on Beacon Hill and home of George Middleton, a colonel in the American Revolution.

3. Phillips School: Corner of Anderson and Pinckney streets. One of the first Boston public schools to admit blacks.

4. John J. Smith home: 86 Pinckney Street. A black abolitionist center and runaway slave meeting place.

Detail from the Shaw Memorial

5. Charles Street Meeting House: Mt. Vernon and Charles streets. Frederick Douglass, Soujourner Truth and Wendall Phillips all spoke here.

6. Lewis & Harriet Hayden House: 66 Phillips Street. An Underground Railroad stop for runaway slaves. Lewis Hayden served in the State Legislature in 1873.

7. Coburn's Gaming House: Phillips and Irving streets

8-12. Smith Court Residences: Homes typical of black residents in the 1800s.

13. Abiel Smith School: 46 Joy Street. A grammar school built in 1834 for black students. Later it was boycotted because of segregation.

14. African Meeting House: 8 Smith Court. The oldest black church building in the US.

Guided Tours

I've included the ones that I think are of special interest to families. There are dozens and dozens of tours around, so make sure you know what you are paying for before you go.

Boston by Little Feet

77 North Washington Street
Boston, MA 02114
617-367-2345
www.bostonbyfoot.com
Tours run May-October, Saturdays and Mondays at 10am; Sundays at 2pm.
Tickets: Adults, $10; children 6-12, $8; children must be accompanied by an adult.

Meet in front of Faneuil Hall, at the statue of Samuel Adams.
Older kids bored by regular tours geared more for adults might enjoy Boston By Little Feet. Targeted for kids ages 6-12, the guides make history fun and adventurous. The tour is a shorter version of the Freedom Trail and kids are invited to answer such

questions as "Why is it nicknamed the French Wedding Cake?" and "More people visit me than Disney World. True or False?" Take the tour to find out the answers. Adults will enjoy it too.

Boston Duck Tours

Administration Office: 790 Boylston Street, MA 02199
617-723-DUCK
www.bostonducktours.com
Tours daily April-November. Ducks leave about every half-hour starting at 9am until an hour before sunset.
Cost: Adult, $24; children 3-11, $15; 3 & under, $3. Tours leave from the Huntington Ave. side of the building and from the Museum of Science.

If you have spent any time in Boston, you'll have noticed the brightly colored odd-looking bus/boats around town. People may

Duck Boats are a big attraction in Boston.

have been making funny noises at you and the driver might have
had something odd on his head, like a Viking Hot. The "buses"
are retired WWII amphibious vehicles reincarnated as tour buses.
They were used to move soldiers and supplies from ships to
beachheads in Europe. Now they are used to move tourists
around in style, in and out of the water. Every conDUCKtor (get
it?) assumes a different character complete with personality.
Your driver might be a Viking or the artist, Vincent Van Duck.
The big draw of the tour is when you leave land behind and
splash into the Charles River. All the children on board are
allowed to steer for a while in the water. Kids will be interested
to know that area schoolchildren named the various Ducks. You
may take a ride in Back Bay Bertha, North End Norma or
Beantown Betty.

The tour hits all the expected tourist sites. Somehow, it just
seems a little more fun when the driver hits the horn and
everyone on board quacks at pedestrians. The entire tour is 80
minutes long, which might make it too long for smaller children.
It runs ran or shine. There is a canopy and the Ducks are heated.
Bundle up in cold weather. It can get chilly on the Charles.
Tickets sell out fast in the summer so it's wise to line up early, as
reservations are not taken. A nice touch is that you can stow
strollers in a safe place by the buses.

Boston History Collaborative
175 Berkeley Street, 3E
617-350-0358
Call for hours and dates of each tour.
They vary and some are given only in the warmer months.

The Boston History Collaborative offers a more in-depth look at
different aspects of Boston and its history. Any of the following
tours designed by them can be done as guided tours, or you can
do it yourself if you get their materials, usually for a fee. Their

website also spells out all the sites on the tours. If you are looking for more than just surface information about Boston, these tours are designed for you.

Boston by Sea – Maritime Trail
Leaves from Long Wharf
www.bostonbysea.org
Adults, $25; children under 12, $10

Take a 90-minute ride around the Boston Harbor and enjoy the performance of costumed actors belting out tunes about Boston's interaction with the sea. The kids will love learning sea shanties (all clean, don't worry). Although it may seem a little goofy, music and costumes get the kids hooked every time. Besides, as long as they get all the facts straight, which they do, why shouldn't learning be fun?

Another option is a free 25-minute guided tour of Long Wharf, also with actors in period costume, sure to interest the kids. This tour leaves from the Marriott Custom House on Lower State Street. You can also conduct your own tour. Visit the website for detailed maps. A few sites you'll visit include Long Wharf, historic piers and the Charlestown Navy Yard.

Literary Trail of Greater Boston
Guided tour: year-round on Saturdays at 9am. (Tours last 3 hours.)
Price: Adults, $30
www.lit-trail.org

The guided tour (transportation provided) starts at the Omni Parker House, where many literati dined and debated, then you're off to visit the Boston Public Library, America's first free municipal library. After that, it's on to Concord to see Emerson's private study; Orchard House, home to Louisa May Alcott and Thoreau's Walden Pond.

You can end the tour in Harvard Square, America's first college, or head back for lunch at the Parker House.

Self-guided tour
Price: $21
For do-it-yourselfers, pay a $21 fee and get the guidebook "The Literary Trail of Greater Boston," by Susan Wilson and the Boston History Collaborative, plus free admission to the Gibson House in Boston and the Orchard House and the Concord Museum in Concord. This is a little easier on the pocketbook than the guided tour, but obviously, you'll need a car.

Innovation Odyssey
Leaves from 28 State Street/Citizens' Bank
www.innovationodyssey.com
Tours on Saturdays at 2pm.
Tickets: $25 for adults; $10 for children under 12.
Take the Orange or Blue Line T to State Street.

This tour is recommended for kids over 10. It's a fascinating look at inventors and sights in Boston where many important discoveries were made. The two-hour tour takes you to Harvard University, the Massachusetts Institute of Technology and what's called "Genetown, USA," (the center of gene research).

You'll see just where Alexander Graham Bell invented the telephone and where modern surgery started at Massachusetts General Hospital. Actors keep things moving along, while teaching you about history.

Kim Foley MacKinnon

Historic Neighborhoods
99 Bedford Street
617-426-1885, www.historic-neighborhoods.org

This is yet another fabulous organization that makes exploring Boston and its history a pleasure, not a chore. Programs include Neighborhood Discovery Walks, Urban Explorer Series, and Ducklings Day Parade. Although these activities may be more interesting or convenient to those who live here, anyone who wants to explore more of Boston than a quick jaunt through town can give you should check out the Neighborhood Discovery Tours. Planning is a little tough since the tours are periodic but call ahead to see what's on offer. HN is the host of the annual Ducklings Days Parade held on Mother's Day, a not-to-miss event if you have young children familiar with the "Make Way for Ducklings" book by Robert McCloskey. This may sound silly but children dress up in their favorite duck outfits and quack their way through Beacon Hill and they've done it annually since 1979. If you want to march in the parade, call to register first.

Old Town Trolleys
7 Commercial Wharf
617-269-7010, www.trolleytours.com
Cost: Adults, $25; under 12, free. Two-day pass: $35.

Hopping on and off the Old Town Trolley is a convenient and easy way to see the city. Sixteen stops hit all the major tourist areas and save you driving and parking. A complete tour without getting off is about two hours. Children will love riding in the trolley and the drivers are all full of lore and funny stories. This is the tour to take if you want to explore parts of the Freedom Trail without wearing out your shoes. There's not a lot of space for strollers, which must be folded up. Try to leave it home or at your hotel if you can.

84

PhotoWalks
617-851-2273, www.photowalks.com
Tours of Beacon Hill, Freedom Trail and Public Garden.
Tickets: $22.

PhotoWalks offers a unique way to sightsee. While walking you through Beacon Hill, along the Freedom Trail or through the Public Garden, reciting history and pointing out attractions, owner Saba Alhadi also instructs guests on great photo opportunities. With a book in hand showing "good" pictures and "bad" ones, she urges her charges to look at the city in a different light.

At the beginning of the tour, she gives a list of hard-to-spot objects to watch out for on the way, to make sure you are paying attention. Alhadi even offers a guide filled with photography tips at the end of the tour. Children on her tours have brought Fisher Price cameras and disposable ones, so even the youngest aspiring photographers can get in the spirit of the tour.

Boston Arts Tours
617-732-3920, www.bostonarttours.com
The Art Tours for Children package is free to children 4-11, with a paying adult ($75, plus entrance fees). Call or view website for other packages.

"Cultural fun with style," is how Marina Veronica describes her very hands-on way of touring any of the city's museums you choose. She gives personalized tours that will make you long for one at every museum you visit. The Art Tours for Children package makes kids think about what they are seeing in a fun, never intimidating, way. While a little pricey, the tour is worth it.

Walking Tours of Historic Boston
617-670-1888, ext.1, www.walkingboston.com
Tickets: adults, $10; children under 12, $6.

Ben Edwards, a descendent of Paul Revere, decided to put the
years of genealogical research he did for his children's historical
fiction book, *One April in Boston*, to another use. Edwards, who
is a board member of the Paul Revere House, details in his book
and on the tour his family's connection to Paul Revere and the
Sons of Liberty. On this three-hour tour Edwards brings some
family artifacts and images to share, which gives a personal touch
and a new meaning to "living history," a popular phrase used in
describing Boston and it attractions.

Women's Heritage Trail
22 Holbrook Street
617-522-2872, www.bwht.org

The Boston Women's Heritage Trail organization grew out of a
program in local schools. Now it sells a guidebook listing all the
sites where women made a difference in Boston, as well as
publishing many self-guided walking tour brochures.

Go to their website and print up a walk that interests you.
Wherever you are in Boston, you can be sure a woman made her
mark nearby. You'll never have enough time to take in all the
sites, but it's worth doing a little research or buying the
guidebook to teach your children about the contributions that
women made that were often overlooked. At the very least, you
can show off while you are sightseeing. Point out where Fannie
Farmer published her first cookbook in 1896 (Boston Cooking
School, 174 Tremont Street), or where the woman who started
"Mother's Day" once lived (15 Pinckney Street.). That woman
was Julia Ward Howe. She also wrote the "Battle Hymn of the
Republic."

Four: On Stage

Theatre & Music

Boston bends over backwards to interest and include children in the fine arts. Almost every venue in town offers special productions, tours and programs with a young audience in mind. Productions are often during the day and much cheaper than regular theatre tickets. And let's face it. If you are a busy parent, you probably don't get to the theatre that much. Taking your kids is a way to expose them to something more enriching than TV and you get to experience some highbrow culture again. Everybody wins. An added bonus is that some of Boston's theatres, such as the Wang and the Shubert are stunningly gorgeous. They are extravagant with gold and ornate decorations that children can appreciate as much as adults.

I've listed only shows and events with children specifically in mind. What this sometimes means is that it's a matinee when the adults in the audience know not to expect utter silence. Remember, you can always just leave if it's too hard for your children to sit still. Before you go, tell your kids about the need to whisper if they just have to talk. Explain the story in detail if you are going to a play and what is going to happen. My five-year-old daughter mistakenly thought she was going to dance in "The Nutcracker," not just see it! It's helpful for children to know what to expect every step of the way.

For more details, call the theatre, or visit each venue's website. Call ahead to the box office and ask if booster seats are allowed. This will save you from having a squirming child (who can't see over the tall person in front of her) in your lap for two hours while you sullenly stare at the empty space next to you now serving as an expensive coat rack. Some theatres even have boosters.

Boston Ballet

19 Clarendon Street (headquarters; performances are usually at the Wang Center, except for The Nutcracker, scheduled to move to the Opera House in 2004)
617-695-6950, www.bostonballet.org
Tickets: $14-65
To the Wang Center: Take the Green Line to the Boylston Street stop.

Boston Ballet's most widely seen show is "The Nutcracker," which has an annual six-week run. More than 140,000 people attend the ever-popular classic and with good reason. Many local aspiring child dancers from the Boston Ballet's Center for Dance Education appear in the production, adding even more charm. One might think that the show would be more of a draw for young girls and their families, but when we went, both boys and girls were decked in their holiday best, equally thrilled. The ballet is a solid two-and-a-half hours, so if you have a squirmer, think twice. Other fairy tales, such as "Sleeping Beauty" and "Cinderella," make ballet appealing to a young audience.

Boston Children's Theatre

The Copley Theatre
225 Clarendon Street
617-424-6634, www.bostonchildrenstheatre.org
Take the Green Line to the Copley Square stop.

"Live Theatre for Children by Children" is the motto of Boston Children's Theatre (BCT), a 75-year-old institution. Students in grades 4-12 perform productions such as "Annie," "The Wizard of Oz" and "The House at Pooh Corner." The BCT also offers classes to students in grades K-12. Performances are geared to ages 4 and up. Most children are natural performers and getting a chance to watch their peers in action often fascinates them.

Boston Symphony Orchestra/Boston Pops Orchestra
Symphony Hall, 301 Massachusetts Avenue
617-266-1492, www.bso.org
Family & Youth concerts: November-April
Admission: $18; tickets often sell out in advance.
Take the Green Line to the Symphony Hall stop.

The Boston Symphony Youth and Family Concerts, held November through April, are a fabulous introduction to the symphony for children. These concerts are also a bargain for music-loving parents. The Youth Concerts are geared for kids over eight or so and are held weekdays, making it easy for schools to take field trips. The Family Concerts are held Saturdays at 10am and noon and are for ages 5 and up. (Children four and under will not be admitted at any time.) The music is chosen with the young audience in mind.

If you attend the 10am concert, you can come in early for an instrument demonstration by the symphony musicians at 9am. After the later performance, tours of Symphony Hall are given. Either of these choices makes the experience a little more hands-on and interesting for children. Youthful Keith Lockhart, besides being the Boston Pops conductor, is also conductor of the Youth Concerts. His presence alone has brought a lot of interest in recent years to the symphony.

Coolidge Corner Theatre (Children's Programs)
290 Harvard Street
Brookline, MA 02445
617-734-2531, www.coolidge.org
Saturday mornings, October-March, at 10:30am;
Admission: Live shows are $8; cartoons, $3. Six shows are $35.
Take the Green Line C train to the Cleveland Circle stop.

The Coolidge, Boston's only remaining open Art Deco movie theater, which is also non-profit, offers a nice change of pace from regular Saturday morning cartoons at home. Every Saturday at 10:30am, a family variety show is offered and it is not restricted to movies. Magic, dance, puppets and classic cartoons are all part of the mix. Before the main production, local kids perform anything from vaudeville to songs, sort of like a mini-talent show. There are contests, giveaways and games. A live ensemble plays tunes kids will recognize, such as songs from Disney movies. The main live show along with classic cartoons is reminiscent of the way movies used to be presented. The program is a full 90 minutes with a 10-minute intermission.

Once Upon A Time's Interactive Shows
The Lyric Stage
140 Clarendon St.
617-437-7172, www.lyricstage.com
Weekends, September-May at 11am.
Tickets: $7 (children under 2, free), reservations recommended.
Take the Orange Line to Back Bay or the Green Line to Copley Square.

Once Upon a Time, a participatory theater company that performs at the Lyric Stage Theatre makes the kids the stars in their shows. At each performance, several random children attending the show are chosen to participate, given costumes, and guided by a couple of actors who narrate a familiar tale while moving the kids through the show. The audience participates as well, encouraged to yell out answers or shout out magic words and the like. It's hard to tell who gets more enjoyment out of the production, the adults or the kids.

For a "Wizard of Oz" production, the roles of the Tin Man, the Cowardly Lion, the Scarecrow, Toto, the munchkins and the monkeys were all available for children. One actress in the theater company played the role of Dorothy, another played Auntie Em, Glenda, the Wicked Witch and Oz. As she acted out the story, she prompted the children with phrases such as "Now the munchkins appeared," and then waved the kids over. Shows are designed for children between the ages of 2 and 8 and the older children are picked to play the larger roles. Each performance is little over an hour and contains popular elements of a tale. Afterwards, the children swarm the stage to meet the actors and pose with them for pictures.

Getting children involved with a production, rather than requiring them to just watch, introduces a sense of fun and accessibility to the theater that may just last a lifetime.

Puppet Showplace Theatre
32 Station Street
Brookline, MA 02445
617-731-6400, www.puppetshowplace.org
Take the Green Line D to Brookline Village. The theatre is across the street.
Performances during the school year are held Saturday & Sunday at 1pm & 3pm, with a preschool show on Thursdays at 10:30am; summer shows are usually held Wednesdays & Thursdays. During school breaks, there are shows daily.
Admission: $8.50 per person for Family Shows

The Puppet Showplace Theatre is a magical experience, but make sure you're kids are up for it. Many smaller children are afraid of puppets. Weekend shows are for 5-year-olds and older. Special "Tot" shows on Thursdays are targeted for the 3-to-5 year old set, where the puppeteers introduce themselves and the stories are more familiar. The theatre is small, with less than 100 seats, so no seat is bad but make sure you get one by reserving well in advance. Tickets sell out all the time. A recent lineup of shows included "Eeore's Birthday," and "Rumplestiltskin." Many days after the shows, the puppeteers will allow children a closer look at the puppets and sometimes (for a fee) you can make your own.

Kim Foley MacKinnon

The Wang Center for the Performing Arts
270 Tremont Street
617-482-9393, www.wangcenter.org
Take the Green Line to the Boylston Street stop.

The Wang Center, considered New England's "grand dame" of theater, opened in 1925. Just visiting the Wang alone is almost worth the price of admission to any of the shows there. It was modeled after the Paris Opera Comique and is simply stunning. Murals, gold leaf, marble columns and intricate carvings make it a feast for the eyes. But guess what? You can also bring the children to see shows such as "Scooby Doo: Stage Fright" and "Blues Clues Live Two!" The Wang offers everything from these obvious children's hits to musicals, dances, concerts and a classic film series in the winter.

Wheelock Family Theatre
180 The Riverway (Wheelock College), Jamaica Plain
617-734-4760, www.wheelock.edu
Tickets $10-17
Three mainstage productions annually.
Take the Green Line D train to the Fenway stop. It's a five-minute walk.

The non-profit Wheelock Family Theatre focuses on shows that everyone can enjoy. Past productions include "The Hobbit," "The Prince and the Pauper," and "The Trumpet and the Swan." The theatre works hard to attract all ages and offers one drama for adults annually, as well as a musical, and a show for both children and adults. Classes for preschoolers on up include dance, beginning Shakespeare, puppetry, drama and much more.

Five: Where to Stay & Eat

A comprehensive listing of restaurants and hotels in the Boston area is beyond the scope of this guide. Since this is a parent-oriented guidebook, I've tried to search out special deals and fun places that have children in mind, or at least places where the staff won't recoil with horror when you walk in the door.

Here's a brief list of some places where being a kid or having a kid is not considered a liability. They are in no special order of preference. I've just listed them alphabetically.

Places to Eat

"Family-Friendly" dining can mean different things to different people. To me, it means a place where the whole family can find something enjoyable about the experience. It is not a place where the parents suffer in silence in a theme-oriented restaurant with dressed up characters and video games (although these do have their place) just for the sake of eating out with the kids. It is also not a place where, should your child decide he'd prefer dining under the table rather than with you, the other patrons would give you the evil eye. The following restaurants have good food and interesting atmospheres or histories that everyone should like.

Bella Luna/Milky Way
403 Centre Street
Jamaica Plain, MA 02130
617-524-5050, www.milkywayjp.com

Bowling and pizza. Fun for the whole family! Ah, but this is no regular bowling alley. Gourmet pizza upstairs in the restaurant Bella Luna and candlepin bowling (smaller pins and balls with no holes if you've never done this) downstairs in the Milky Way lounge. You can also eat downstairs in the bar area before bowling. Pizza is served on plastic plates that were decorated by kids. You know the ones. You probably did this as a kid or have done it with your own kids. The bar area is awash with funky lights and solar system sculptures. I had my 30th birthday party here, with many children accompanying parents, and we all had a blast. There are ball ramps to put in the alley so kids can definitely knock down some pins. Private parties are common on the weekends so call ahead if you want to bowl. Kids have to be 48 inches tall to play.

Durgin Park

340 Faneuil Hall Marketplace
617-227-2038
Open daily 11:30am-10pm; Fri. & Sat. until 10:30pm, Sundays 1:30-9pm.
Take the Green Line T to Government Center. Cross City Hall Plaza.

No guidebook would be complete without including Durgin Park. This restaurant, open since 1827, is one of the last places in town to get Indian pudding and true Boston baked beans. It is always busy and packed with tourists. Kids like sitting at the picnic tables. The portions are huge and prices are cheap so this is good bet for a decent family meal. Just don't look for anyone to hold your hand here – the waitstaff is not known for its friendliness. It's almost a point of pride.

Full Moon

344 Huron Avenue
Cambridge, MA 02138
617-354-6699
& 138 Mass. Ave., Arlington, 781-646-1404
Open: Mon-Fri, 10am-3pm and 5pm-9pm; brunch weekends 9am-3pm. Kids' cooking classes also occasionally offered with parent.

This is such a wonderful place! In my world, every town would have one. Toys, mac-n-cheese, sippy cups if you forgot yours. You are thinking "What's so great about that? I can just stay at home."

Sadie enjoys mac-n-cheese at Full Moon.

Well, this restaurant also has gourmet food for the grown-ups. You can have a glass of wine, a delicious salad, and steak, while the kids play nearby. You can probably even finish your dinner without interruption. And the kids love their food too. All kid dishes come with carrot sticks and cut up fruit. The portions are generous and one grown-up I go with usually ends up eating part of her daughter's mac-and-cheese; it's that good.

There's a train set up, kitchen, dollhouse and more. Or, kids can bring a bucket of toys to the table with them. For budding chefs in the family, find out when parent and child cooking classes are held. Maybe your kids will make gourmet meals for you someday. A word to the wise: Try not to come right at midday. The place is packed, with good reason. If you come around 1pm, things are usually a bit calmer and you don't have to play referee in the toy area with all the children competing for space.

Grill 23
161 Berkeley St., Copley Square
617-542-2255
Take the Green Line T to Copley.

It's fancy, to be sure. This steakhouse in the former Salada Tea building is a bastion of brass, white tablecloths and beef. But, if you are in the mood for a special night out, there are options for kids. The mac-n-cheese (listed as a side dish for $12) is sublime. Four cheeses and truffle oil are just part of the recipe.

Johnny's Luncheonette
Harvard Square
1105 Massachusetts Avenue
Cambridge, MA 02138
617-495-0055
Open: 8 am-10 pm
Take the Red Line T to Harvard Square.

This re-creation of a '50s diner is a much better choice than nearby chains or fast food in Harvard Square. Right on the menu it states, "We love kids." When you sit down, the waitstaff presents a toy to keep kids busy until the food comes. Old-fashioned frappes (milkshakes, for those not familiar with the term) are huge and delicious. Obviously, burgers are big here and the sweet potato fries are outstanding. Breakfast can be ordered all day. They also have great meatloaf. Healthy alternatives are an option.

Kingfish Hall
188 Faneuil Hall South Market Building
617-523-8862
Take the Green Line T to Government Center.

The décor of this Todd English property is a lot of fun, with art installations and swirling lights, sure to catch your kids' eyes. They have a children's menu with a choice of beverages, entrees and ice cream ($8.95). Seafood is the specialty. Service is great and very friendly.

Marche Movenpick
Prudential Center, 800 Boylston Street
617-578-9700, www.marcheusa.com
Open: 7:30am-2 am
Take the Green Line to the Hynes/ICA stop.

Grab your passport and tour the world. Okay, tour the world's food. At Marche Movenpick, you are handed a passport when you enter the restaurant/cafeteria, then you can visit any number of food stations. Whatever you pick will be recorded on your passport, which is then used to tally up the price of your meal. Watch chefs prepare your meal right on the spot. Kids like the freedom and the responsibility of deciding what they want to eat, although don't be surprised if they head straight for the pizza chef, conveniently located right next to the small two-room play area. (It's too bad the play area isn't set up so more tables can see it; adults have to stand nearby to keep an eye on their kids.) You'll probably pay more than you would at the food court on the other side of the mall, but you'll get much better food. Everything looks so tempting; it's easy to load up your tray with more than you'll eat. They also have a food shop downstairs where you can pack a mighty tempting picnic.

North End (anywhere)
Take the Green line T to North Station.

Kids and pasta (not to mention gelato) were made for each other. The one problem with eating in the North End is deciding where to go. Every place tempts you with delicious smells wafting through the doorway. Every pastry shop window seems to have your kids' name written on it. Pizzeria Regina on Thatcher Street is always a good choice. Pitchers of soda, a family atmosphere and big tables make this Boston restaurant an institution. Hanover Street is the main drag. Dozens of restaurants and bakeries can be found here and on numerous side streets.

Quincy Market
Congress Street
617-338-2323, www.fanueilhallmarketplace.com
Take the Green Line T to Government Center.

Quincy Market has more than 40 food stalls and plenty of restaurants. Take your pick from pizza, hot dogs, stuffed potatoes, clam chowder and more. You can eat at little café tables, find a sit-down restaurant, or grab a stroller (sandwich) and head outside if it's nice.

Redbones
55 Chester Street
Somerville, MA 02144
617-628-2200
Open 11:30am-11:30 pm. Cash only accepted.
Take the Red Line T to Davis Square.

Messy, loud and delicious. If you like BBQ – real BBQ, not sauce out of a bottle – go to Redbones. The kids will like all the funky decorations and finger food. You'll like the casual atmosphere. Even vegetarians can make a meal here out of corn fritters, rice and beans and delicious cornbread. Drinks come in big mugs and the waitstaff is always friendly. You may have to wait for a table, and don't forget, cash only. (If you do forget anyway, an ATM is just down the street. We've had to run down there more than once.)

Tremont 647
647 Tremont Avenue
617-266-4600
Pajama Brunch Sundays. 10:30am-3pm.

On Sunday mornings, the staff wears pajamas and encourages the patrons to do so too. This is a fun way to start off Sunday. Roll out of bed and go get breakfast. You may feel a little silly, but believe me, you get over it fast and the kids love it. It's very popular, so get there early or be prepared to wait. At least you'll be comfortable. The menu is a la carte. The upscale restaurant is probably not a good spot for children except for the Sunday brunch.

Union Oyster House
Government Center & the North End/Faneuil Hall
41 Union Street
617-227-2750, www.unionoysterhouse.com
On the Freedom Trail, one block from Faneuil Hall
Open Sun.-Thurs, 11am-9:30pm; Fri. & Sat. 11am-10pm. Reservations recommended.
Take the Blue or Green Line to Government Center. Cross Congress Street. You'll see the sign for the restaurant.

The Union Oyster House was established in 1826. It's near the Faneuil Hall area, making it an easy tourist stop. Don't let the obviousness of the attraction scare you away. It's a pretty neat place and if your kids won't eat oysters, don't worry, there's plenty else to choose from on the kid's menu. Hamburgers, spaghetti and grilled cheese, children's staples, are all available. You must get a side order of Boston Baked Beans – they are delicious.

Upstairs on the Square
91 Winthrop St., Harvard Square, Cambridge.
617-864-1933, www.upstairsonthesquare.com
Take the Red Line T to Harvard Square

The Monday Club, the casual dining area of the restaurant, is the spot to take the kids. They won't know where to look first, what with a pink ceiling, purple tables, zebras in tutus and huge ornate mirrors. The food here is simply amazing, as is the service, and for kids to eat, there is a grilled cheese of the day and a special request for mac-n-cheese is always granted.

Zon's
2 Perkins St., Jamaica Plain
617-524-9667

Okay. Not one, not two, but three different versions of mac-n-cheese can be found on Zon's menu! How can you go wrong? There's regular ($12); mac & cheese & peas ($14); and the mac daddy that comes with grilled chorizo sausage ($14). This cozy (but dark) restaurant is a good choice for families earlier in the evening, before it gets too crowded. Lots of other comfort food for adults, too, like meatloaf and chicken pot pie.

Places to Stay

Packages are often the way to go with kids. Most of them offer a bunch of free things. Complimentary tickets, meals and parking offered can end up saving you a lot of money. And, if you're a townie, don't ignore this section. Kids love hotels. They have neat little bars of soap and the ice machines are always lots of fun. Maybe everyone could use a night away from home, even if it is just across town. A new perspective on your city can be gained when you leave the mundane everyday world behind for the weekend.

Many hotels let kids under 12 stay free in the parent's room. Some offer a second, connected room, at half-price for families. Check out www.bostonusa.com for deals.

Boston Harbor Hotel

70 Rowes Wharf
800-752-7077, www.bhh.com

The Boston Harbor Hotel is right on Rowes Wharf. You can walk to Faneuil Hall, the Freedom Trail and the Aquarium. The Family Getaway Vacation Package includes accommodations for two adults and two children, breakfast for four in your room or in the restaurant, coloring books and crayons, four tickets to the New England Aquarium, free valet parking and use of the heath club. In addition, you have the use of cribs, strollers and games, which can all be brought to the room. The Boston Harbor Hotel also has babysitting available for an extra cost.

The Colonnade

120 Huntington Avenue
617-424-7000; 800-962-3030, www.colonnadehotel.com

A great location, fabulous restaurant (Brasserie Jo), and interesting packages make this a fun choice. In the summer, there's the only city-view rooftop pool in Boston to swim in. The "Kids See & Do" weekend package includes a one-night stay in a deluxe guestroom, four passes (2 adults/2 children) to the New

England Aquarium or the Children's Museum, full American breakfast at Brasserie Jo (in the hotel), overnight parking and late checkout (2pm).

In the winter, the Colonnade has a clever weekend package called "Frosty Fridays." On Fridays, between November 23 and March 29, you pay whatever the temperature is outside. This could mean you pay just $10 if it's 10 degrees at 5pm, when the official temperature for the night is taken. However, there is a catch: Your required Saturday night stay costs the going rate.

The package also includes ice-skate rentals and tickets for the Boston Common Frog Pond for two or tickets for the Old Town Trolley, plus French hot cocoa for two at Brasserie Jo and overnight parking.

Hyatt Regency Cambridge
575 Memorial Drive
Cambridge, MA 02139
800-233-1234, www.cambridge.hyatt.com

The "Family Getaway" package includes a deluxe guestroom, 50 percent off an adjoining or connecting room, and a host of complimentary features such as a kid's gift bag, continental breakfast for four in Zephyr on the Charles, bike rentals for four (seasonally) for one hour, in-room movie, popcorn and soda, parking, access to the indoor pool. The view over the Charles River is beautiful. The Spinnaker Restaurant, located in the hotel, offers great food, along with stunning views. There is a scheduled shuttle to Boston so the Cambridge location isn't inconvenient for tourists.

Royal Sonesta Hotel Boston
5 Cambridge Parkway, Cambridge
617-806-4200, www.sonesta.com

The hotel offers a "Family Fun Weekend package," which includes four passes to the Museum of Science or Children's Museum, cookies and milk at bedtime, use of the indoor pool, and during the summer, use of bicycles, boat rides and ice cream are complimentary. A unique feature of the hotel is the stellar artwork found throughout the lobby. A self-guided tour with a headset is offered. The best part for families is that it's next door to the Museum of Science, which is great.

Seaport Hotel
One Seaport Lane, Boston,
877-SEAPORT, www.seaporthotel.com

The "Children's Weekend Adventure" package includes room, four passes to the Children's Museum and use of the indoor pool. Bonus: the museum is within walking distance. Aura, the hotel's restaurant, has wonderful food and a great kids' menu.

Boston skyline

Six: Day Trips

If you never left Boston's city limits, you'd have enough to keep you busy for years, but there are many important and interesting sites nearby. If you want to see where the Puritans first landed, you'll have to go south to Plymouth. Concord and Lexington, with the North Bridge and the Lexington Green, with Boston, set the stage for the American Revolution. Salem or "Witch City" is a big lure year-round (not just at Halloween) and besides fascinating the children with its grisly past, the town is a wonderful place to explore. You have to leave Boston and head west if you want to lost in a giant maze in a corn field or to visit the first polar bear born in New England.

Day trips usually mean car trips but some places are easy to get to by train. My usual criterion for a day trip is that it has to be less than a two-hour drive each way. Most of these sights are actually less than an hour, making them more of a morning or afternoon trip, but I have included a few that are longer because they shouldn't be missed.

North

Salem
Salem is located 16 miles north of Boston. It's easy to drive or take the train to Salem. Once there, you don't need a car. It's a very walkable city.

By car
Take Route 128 North to exit 25A and follow Route 114 East into Salem. Follow signs to the Salem Visitor Center, Museum and Historic Sites and Downtown parking.

By train

Take the MBTA Newburyport/Rockport commuter rail train from North Station to the Salem depot. It's a five-minute walk to the Visitor Center (59 Wharf St; 877-SALEMMA).

Salem is an eclectic mix of true historical sites (such as the House of Seven Gables) cheesy museums (the Museum of Myths & Monsters), and modern-day witches (who proudly proclaim their wiccan colors). It's fun to explore this waterfront town, with its neat gift shops and seafood restaurants.

I've listed a few places you shouldn't miss if you are visiting Salem. Wandering around on your own, you'll find a lot more to experience. Salem has its own heritage trail to follow around, just like Boston, and it is painted red too. Stop in at the Visitor Center for a map.

Salem Witch Museum

Washington Square
Salem, MA 01970
879-744-1692, www.salemwitchmuseum.com
Open: 10am-5pm, daily. Open until 7pm in July and August.
Admission: Adult, $6.50; children, $4.50.

The museum is a mini-education about the witch hysteria of 1692. Thirteen (yes, unlucky 13) stage sets display the story of what really happened in Salem when 19 hapless souls lost their lives to the hysteria of the times. The somewhat cheesy presentation might at times be scary for the little ones. Another exhibit, called "Witches, Evolving Perceptions," will set you and your kids straight on the truth about witches and their religion.

The House of the Seven Gables Historic Site

54 Turner Street
Salem, MA 01970
978-744-0991, wwww.7gables.org
Open: February-June, Monday-Saturdays, 10am-5pm and Sundays, noon-5pm.
Open later July-Oct., until 7pm; Nov. and Dec. hours are 10am-5pm. Closed
the first three weeks of January.
Admission: Adults, $10; children, 6-17, $6.50; under 5, free.

The House of the Seven Gables Historic Site also includes
Nathaniel Hawthorne's Birthplace, the Retire Beckett House, the
Hooper-Hathaway House and a Counting House. Your admission
allows you to roam around them all. The kids all love the secret
staircase in the House of the Seven Gables, which was used to
hide supposed witches, and later, runaway slaves. Combine this
visit with one to the living history museum, Salem 1630: Pioneer
Village and get a sense of what life was like in the 17th century.

Parlee Farms

Farwell Road
Tyngsboro, MA 01879
978-649-3854, www.parleefarm.com
Call for times. They change seasonally.

Parlee Farms makes a delightful family outing, with something
for everyone: a variety of fruits and flowers for picking, a clean
and well-arranged farm animal petting zoo, a fun Hay Play Area,
a demonstration beehive, and an attractive farm stand. Three
generations of my family were thrilled to find plentiful
raspberries and strawberries, as well as autumnal apples and
pumpkins, on a mid-September afternoon. The farm uses
ladybugs, rather than pesticides to control insects, so you can let
the kids snack in the fields without worrying about harmful
poisons. This is a better fall excursion, rather than summer, since

heat makes picking a lot less fun. However, during the summer season a free hayride takes you from one field to the next, which kids always like (what is it about hay, anyway?).

Stone Zoo
149 Pond Street
Stoneham, MA 02180
781-438-5100, www.zoonewengland.com
Open: April-September, 10am-5pm (weekends and holidays open until 6 pm); October-March, open daily 10am-4pm.
Admission: Adults, $6, children 2-15, $3.50; under 2, free.

The Stone Zoo, sister to Boston's Franklin Park Zoo, doesn't have as much to offer as a zoo, but there is an annual event here not to be missed. It's called Zoolights and is held every December. Thousands and thousands of lights make a magical land between 5-9 pm. Santa is on hand to greet visitors (and pose for photos). You'll head down Snowy Owl Creek trail and be enchanted by all the animals, real and fake. Every year it seems the zoo adds new features. The latest attraction is a carousel and kiddie rides. (Admission to Zoolights is $3; under 2, free.)

If you're not here for the lights, you must be here for the animals. There's a barnyard area for petting goats and sheep. The "Snowy Owl Creek" exhibit allows you to view animals not found at many other zoos. Look for snowy owls, lynx, artic foxes and reindeer.

West

If you are doing the history thing with your kids, you'll definitely want to head to Concord and Lexington for the other part of the story. While many exciting events occurred in Boston, you have travel a bit to see the North Bridge, where "the shot heard around the world," happened and the Lexington Battle Green.

I have put various sites in the two towns at the beginning of this section, so you can plan a day trip around visiting more than one attraction. Other points west follow.

In addition to all the history you'll absorb, both towns are beautiful and full of quaint shops and restaurants. Walking around in the fall is particularly spectacular. There's a visitor's center both in Lexington (781-862-1450; www.lexington-chamber.org) and Concord (978-369-3120; www.Lexington-corcord.org) that can help you with maps and other information. Special tours and re-enactments are common.

Concord Museum
200 Lexington Road (Entrance on Cambridge Tpke.)
Concord, MA 01742
978-369-9763, www.concordmuseum.org
Open: Jan.-March, Monday-Saturday, 110am-4pm; Sunday, 1-4pm; April-December, Monday-Saturday, 9-5; Sunday, noon-5.
Admission: Adults, $8; children 6-17, $5. There's a discount for AAA members.

The Concord Museum was established in 1886 and is full of artifacts dating to the 17th century. The lantern that hung in the Old North Church the night of Paul Revere's ride is here as well as items from the American Revolution. The "Why Concord?" exhibit is very informative and details Concord's place in history. Your kids might not be thrilled that the museum has the "world's largest collection of Thoreau possessions," but there are other things to interest them. Pick up an activity pack when you come in to help you explore. The backpack includes reproduced artifacts such as a spy glass, quill, and slate (and much more) and a trail guide. It has directions, a treasure hunt and fun games related to exhibits. Kids eat this stuff up.

The "Artifacts of Childhood" exhibit should also grab kids' attention, showing a glimpse rarely seen into earlier eras of childhood. A children's story hour is held every fourth Friday of the month October-May for kids ages 3-5 at 1pm. Not only is there a story but also a snack and a hands-on activity. The cost is $9 per child (adult, free). Sundays are sometimes "Family Sampler Sundays" with tours and activities. For Massachusetts residents, the "Be Our Guest" program during the winter offers free museum admission for various communities. Check for dates.

Minute Man National Historical Park/North Bridge Minute Man Visitor Center

174 Liberty Street
Concord, MA 01742
978-369-6993, www.nps.gov/mima
Open weekends in December-March from noon to 4pm;
from April-October, 9am-5pm. In November, from 9am-4pm.

The North Bridge, of course, is where "the shot heard 'round the world" took place. You can walk over it and see the "Minute Man Statue" commemorating the events that famous day of April 19, 1775. Start off at the visitor's center for a theater program and brochures. Only the most active or ambitious families will follow the 5.5-mile-long Battle Road Trail, but even walking part of it is a lovely stroll.

Orchard House

399 Lexington Road
Concord, MA 01742
978-369-4118, www.louisamayalcott.org
Open: Apr.-Oct., 10am-4:30pm & Sun. 1-4pm; Nov.-Mar., Mon.-Fri., 11am-3pm; Sat., 10-4:30 pm; Sun., 1-4:30pm. Tours are guided only and given on the half-hour. Call before you go because they sell out when they have groups. Admission: Adults, $8; children, 6-17, $5; family rate (2 adults, 4 kids, $20).

If you are familiar with Little Women, you may want to visit the house where it is believed author Louisa May Alcott set the book. If you take the Literary Trail tour, you'll come by on your tour. The house is much like it was where the Alcotts, all ahead of their time, lived from 1858-1877.

Orchard House usually has a few special events a month, many geared towards families. The "Hand-in-Hand at Orchard House" is an example of a program for children under six with a parent. A tour, dressing up in Victorian clothes, games and songs are all part of the fun.

Old Manse
269 Monument Street
Concord, MA 01742
978-369-3909
Open: Mid-April-October, Monday-Saturday, 10am-5pm;
Sunday and holidays, noon- 5pm.
Admission: Adults, $7.50; ages 6-12, $5; family, $22.

The Old Manse, home to Ralph Waldo Emerson, was built by his grandfather William Emerson in 1770. The North Bridge, which is nearby, is visible from the upstairs rooms. The elder Emerson wrote about the famous events that occurred here. Many years later his grandson wrote "Nature" here.

Later still, Nathaniel Hawthorne and his wife lived here as well, and were very happy. You can see where they scratched their names and little messages to each other in windowpanes throughout the house. This is one of the stops on the Literary Trail. If you are going to visit the North Bridge anyway, stop in.

Walden Pond State Reservation
915 Walden Street
Concord, MA 01742
978-369-3254, www.state.ma.us/dem/parks/wldn.htm
Open dawn to dusk.
Admission: $5 per car

This is one of my absolute favorite day trips. And I'm not the only one who counts this as a great destination, especially in the summer, when if you get here too late, you're out of luck. When the parking lot fills up, no one else is allowed in. So get here early, bring a lunch and an umbrella and prepare to relax. Swimming in Henry David Thoreau's former backyard is a joy for parents and their children. Lifeguards parole a roped-off area on a small beach where most families park themselves. The shallow water extends for several feet and allows little ones to splash around in safety. You can swim beyond the ropes if you want but they make a good boundary for the children. If you want to get out of the water, take a walk around the pond.

A bathhouse makes changing clothes convenient. About the only food around is an ice-cream truck usually parked in the parking lot, so be sure to bring food and water if you'll be here for a while. Although the pond has a lot of shade, it's all away from the beach area. Bring an umbrella. Occasionally the park rangers host activities for children outside the water. One day we visited, my daughter brought home a sun catcher she made with an old CD and beads. If you get tired of swimming or you're a big Thoreau fan, visit the replica of Thoreau's cabin. It's by the parking lot. Rangers give talks in the summer.

Lexington Battle Green
Bedford & Massachusetts Avenue
Lexington, MA
781-862-1450

You might want to start off at the Camber of Commerce Visitor's Center where there is a diorama of the battle and all sorts of information on where the first skirmish of the American Revolution occurred. (Don't be confused by all the firsts everywhere. There are different shades of meaning to them all.) On the Green, there's a statue of Captain Parker and the Revolutionary Monument. You can also see the Old Belfry that alerted the militia.

Museum of Our National Heritage
33 Marrett Road/Route 2A
Lexington, MA
781-861-6559, www.monh.org

To get a more detailed look at what happened in Lexington, you should visit the Museum of Our National Heritage. The permanent exhibit "Lexington Alarm'd" is filled with everything you'd ever wanted to know about that fateful day. Hands-on exhibits should interest the kids. The Museum doesn't limit itself to just this one event. There are many other permanent and special exhibits focusing on everything from clocks to items made in Massachusetts.

Family programs here are very hands-on and lots of fun for kids. One recent family day was tied into an exhibit on milk delivery in New England (don't laugh, it was really neat!). We churned butter, made milk paint and a cow puppet. It was just $5 for the family. Other programs like children's workshops and lectures are offered.

The Butterfly Place
120 Tyngsboro Road
Westford, MA 01886
978-392-0955, www.butterflyplace-ma.com
Open: March 1-Columbus Day 10am-5pm
Admission: adults, $7.50; children, 3-12, $5.50; under 2, free.

Clearly, this is another destination with one thing as its specialty. The Butterfly Place, with its 27-foot atrium holding as many as 500 butterflies at once, is both interesting and beautiful – if you're into butterflies. Don't bring kids here thinking they'll immediately be transfixed. Children under three have to be in a stroller, backpack or held by the hand at all times. An introductory video, display cases and observation room supplement the atrium. Pick up a Papillon Hatching Kit in the gift shop and let the kids watch their own caterpillar turn into a butterfly at home.

Davis' Farmland & Mega Maze
Redstone Hill
Sterling, MA 01564
978-422-MOOO; 978-422-8888
www.davisfarmland.com; www.davismegamaze.com
Farmland: Open weather permitting, April 12-Sept. 3, daily 9:30am-4:30pm; Sep. 6- October, Thurs.-Sun., same hours.
Mega Maze: Open weather permitting, Mid-July through Sept. 3, daily 10am-5pm; Sept.-Oct, weekends only.
Admission to Farmland: General admission, $11; under 2, free. Mega Maze: Adults, $10.95; kids under 14, $8.95; under 4, free. Combo pass to both is available.

This place is so much fun that you'll forgive the hour-plus it takes to get here. If you have a mixed-age group you can always visit both the Farmland and the Mega Maze – plan on a full day to do both. The complex is run by seventh-generation Davis' family members. When farming wasn't making money for them anymore, they turned the land into a more profitable venture. Lucky for us they did.

The Farmland is the perfect size for a grand younger kid adventure. They say they cater to the under-eight set here but I'm guessing older kids will like the animals too. Children are encouraged to go right into most of the animal pens if they like. We spent a good half-hour watching as our daughter hugged all the little kids (goats, that is) she could find. The Farm is more than a mere petting zoo though. It is home to many rare endangered species of livestock, which the Davis' are trying to breed to save them from extinction. There is a concession stand and picnic area.

The Mega Maze is definitely geared more for adults and older kids. It's an amazing example of what you can do with a tractor and a cornfield. Each year a master maze maker from England redesigns the maze and it takes on a new theme. One year it was in the shape of a UFO. The following year it was a T-Rex. There are always several ways to solve the maze but don't worry if you can't. There are friendly maze guides on patrol to point you in the right direction (and they never lie). Make sure your kids are up for the challenge. It can be a little claustrophobic and being stuck in a cornfield with a screaming toddler is no fun. Stick to the Farmland if you think that might be a problem.

DeCordova Museum and Sculpture Park

51 Sandy Pond Road
Lincoln, MA 01773
781-259-8355
www.decordova.org
Open: Tues.-Sun., 10am-5pm. Sculpture Park open daily.
Admission: Adults, $6; children 6-12, $4; 5 and under, free.

This museum is great fun, especially for kids who get itchy in museums. Examining the more than 70 outdoor sculptures is definitely an adventure and they'll like the fact that no one is warning them not to touch. They are even encouraged to pick up sticks from the grounds and play on a giant xylophone.

Modern and contemporary art are the focus of the museum, which was formerly the estate of Julian de Cordova.

Fun at the DeCordova Museum in Lincoln.

Discovery Museums
177 Main Street
Acton, MA 01720
978-264-4201, www.discoverymuseums.org
Call for times. They change seasonally and sometimes groups book the space.
Admission: $8 for one museum; $12 for both.

This duo is a sure-fire winner for residents tired of the city and looking for something different to do. As a tourist, you probably wouldn't want to make a special trip. Visitors to one museum will definitely want to go to the other so buy the $10 ticket up front. The Children's Museum is pretty small and only limited numbers of people are allowed in at one time. I love this policy. There's never a chance of the overcrowding which is often an issue at other museums. If you can't get in right away, there's always room at the much bigger Science Museum next door.

The Children's Museum is like a giant doll's house, or the house your kids would design if you'd let them. Each room explores a different theme. There's the Train Room, Bessie's Play Diner, Woodland Room and several others. You get the picture. This is definitely designed for younger children.

The Science Museum is geared toward older children but my preschooler and her friend enjoyed it too. They wanted to get their little hands on the tools in the Inventor's Workshop (you have to be six for that exhibit). Instead, they contented themselves with percussion instruments in the Music Room.

My major complaint about the Discovery Museums is that there is no lunchroom area. There are picnic tables outside, but these work only in nice weather. So if you are here during lunchtime, you either have to sneak your lunch in a staircase like we did, eat in the car or head home.

Drumlin Farm Wildlife Sanctuary

South Great Road, Route 117
Lincoln, MA 01773
617-259-9807, www.massaudubon.org
Open: March-October, Tuesday-Sunday 9am-5pm and Monday holidays; November-February, closes at 4pm.
Admission: Adults, $6; children 3-12, $4 (free to Mass Audubon Society members)

The Massachusetts Audubon Society runs this 250-acre working farm which is home to pigs, cows, horses – the works. The ubiquitous hayride is available for $1. In addition to the old favorites, there is the Burrowing Animal Building, with foxes and woodchucks; trails to explore; and gardens to poke around in. A gift shop and small farm stand are located near the entrance.

Myriad programs and demonstrations are held throughout the year. Examples include helping the farmers in the "See How it Grew" program, where kids and their parents help put the farm's garden to rest in the winter. In the fun "Farmers" Helper" program kids help with milking, collecting eggs and other farmyard chores. There are eight-week programs, but many one-day lectures and other events may coincide with a visit.

Ecotarium

222 Harrington Way
Worcester, MA 01604
508-929-2700, www.ecotarium.org
Open: Tuesday-Saturday,10am-5pm; noon-5pm, Sunday. Open Monday holidays.
Admission: Adults, $8; children, 3-16, $6; under 3, free. Express train tickets, $2. On the first Sunday of every month, admission is free from 12-5pm.
From Boston, take the Mass Pike West to Exit 11. Take a left on Route 122 North. Go 3 miles and take a right on Plantation Street. Go 1 mile to Franklin Street and take a right. Take the second right onto Harrington Way.

Many people have problems with zoos, with animals used as displays to entertain. If you feel that way, but still like to see wild creatures up close, this is the place for you. The Ecotarium has a raise-and-release program and houses animals that can't live in the wild for whatever reason. Some have been injured or are ill, others have had too much contact with humans to make it alone in the wild. Kendra the polar bear is a huge draw, as she was born here in 1984 and is the first polar bear born in New England to survive. Annually, red-bellied turtles spend winter at the Ecotarium and then are released in spring. Permanent residents include bald eagles, otters and bobcats.

The Explorer Express Train (additional $2) takes visitors through the grounds in a mini-copy of an 1860s steam engine train. The Preschool Room is stocked with activities, books, and ferrets and makes a nice stop with those with children under 5. Children can look through giant microscopes or listen to animal sounds on earphones. The Planetarium ($2.50 admission) offers all sorts of interesting programs, including one that looks into what the stars meant to Native Americans and Ancient Greeks.

It may seem that every time you turn around, you're asked to pay another fee but it's all for a good cause. And truly, this is a unique place. You're not going to find many sites where you can actually explore the treetops. In fact, you won't find any others in this country. The exhibit, for those not afraid of heights, is called the Tree Canopy Walkway (kids must be seven or older, accompanied by an adult). A series of cable walkways suspended 40 feet up is modeled after those in tropical rainforests and allows you to explore a region usually reserved for the birds. Don't worry, you don't have to go it alone. This is an hour-long guided exhibit and you must register in advance. You'll be harnessed up, complete with helmet, and up you go, eye-level with many creatures you'd never see down below.

Nashoba Valley Winery

100 Wattaquadoc Hill Road
Bolton, MA 01740
978-779-5521, www.nashobawinery.com
Open year-round. Call to find out what's in season.
Take the Mass Pike West to 495 North. Take exit 17 (Route 117 West) and go
1 mile to Bolton Center. Turn left on Wattaquadoc Hill Road (blinking light).
The Winery is 1/4 down on the right. It's less than 40 minutes from Boston.

Don't get nervous. I'm not throwing caution to the wind and getting the toddlers tipsy. Nashoba Valley Winery is much more than a winery. At least 100 varieties of apples are grown here, waiting for you to pick them in season, as well as plums, raspberries, strawberries, peaches and more. All this fruit is used in the different varieties of wines Nashoba produces, but you can have the fruit in its purest form, freshly plucked. And if you get tired before you have enough to take home, you can take the easy way out and do your picking from bushels.

We make an annual pilgrimage in the fall and attend either the Harvest Festival in September or their Oktoberfest. Along with the apple picking there's music, entertainment and food. It is such a beautiful setting that it's easy to just hang out all day. Call to get the season's schedules for fruit picking. There's also a store if you want to take home some of the Winery's wares or locally produced condiments and a restaurant open for lunch and dinner.

Old Sturbridge Village

One Old Sturbridge Village Road, Route 20
Sturbridge, MA 01566
508-347-3363, www.osv.org
Open daily in April from 9:30am-4pm; May-October, 9:30am-5pm; November-March, call for times.
Admission: Adults, $20; children 3-17, $5; under 3, free. Tickets are good for two consecutive days.

Old Sturbridge Village a living history museum permanently set in the years 1790 to 1840. Living history museums can go either way for kids. Either the novelty of people in period costume speaking in dialect is fun and novel or it's a bore. Sturbridge Village is very large, with more than 40 buildings, plus animals, and lots of hands-on activities. It usually has a lot going on so you're bound to find something to entertain the kids, no matter their age.

When you get your ticket, you'll receive a map and a list of that day's events. After the orientation program, you can plan the rest of your visit. You'll definitely need at least a few hours. The Samson's Children's Museum should be the first stop for those with smaller children. A dress-up area, play kitchen, schoolroom are all inviting places to play and not a heavy-handed way to learn about the past. In the warmer months, a ride on the Quinebag River is a treat (costs $3; under 3, free).

There are plenty of choices for eating, from a cafeteria to a tavern or a café, or you can bring your own picnic. On the day you visit you may be able to watch a 19th century magic show or drop in for games at the Town Pound. Periodically, there are special dinner events at Sturbridge Village. For example, you can come to Families Cook, an event where you prepare dinner by the hearth with the costumed interpreters assisting you. A calendar of events listed on the website is helpful to look at when planning your visit. For additional fees, there are hands-on activities for children such as making wood toys or learning how to stencil. You don't have to get too hung up on planning unless there is something specific you want to do. There is usually a wide variety of options on any given day. People who live in the area with children ages 8-12 should check out the Kids Club. It costs $10 for a one-year membership, which allows the child free unlimited admission when accompanied by an adult; a quarterly newsletter; and discounts on activities at the Village.

Kim Foley MacKinnon

South

Edaville Railroad
Route 58
South Carver, MA
508-866-8190; 877-EDAVILLE, www.edaville.org
Open: June-Oct., daily 10am-5pm; Nov.-Jan., Mon.-Fri., 4-9pm, Sat. & Sun. 2-9pm.
Admission: Summer/Fall: Adults, $12.50; children 3-12, $8.50; under 3, free.
Holiday Festival of Lights rates, Nov. 9-Jan. 6: adults, $15; children, $10.

Edaville Railroad takes you on a nostalgic trip back to old-fashioned amusements. Ride the old-timey carousel, watch the smaller children enjoy the kiddie rides and by all means, jump on board the authentic two-foot narrow-gauge railway. Steam and diesel locomotives pull passenger cars on a 5.5-mile trip through 1,800 acres of cranberry bogs. (Everything is included in the admission price.) A playground area with wooden train cars is fun for the little ones and you can climb in old train car engines near the railway as well as an old fire engine.

The Christmas Light Festival is a big draw here, when the place gets gussied up as a winter wonderland, but any time is fun. It's definitely worth the drive from Boston if you live here. If you are just visiting for a few days, you might not want to dedicate the time it takes to get here and back.

Plimoth Plantation & the *Mayflower II*
508-746-4978, www.plimoth.org
Open March-November, 9am-5pm.
Admission: Combo pass (good for two days) for Plimoth Plantation & *Mayflower II*, adult, $22; child, $14. Plantation-only ticket: adult, $20; child, $12. *Mayflower II* only: adult, $8; child, $6. Under 5, free.

122

Plimoth Plantation

Visit the year 1627 in this re-creation of a Pilgrim village (about 20 structures) and Hobbamock's (Wampanoag Indian) Homesite. Trained staff dress and speak as though they were in the 17th century. It amuses some kids, and adults too, to try to trip up the Pilgrims with modern-day questions but they are too well trained. They'll give you a puzzled look if you ask what kind of computer they use. This living history museum is a great way to impart an important part of our past. The staff can tell you how they cook on a hearth or how difficult the winters are, all in period dialect. In Hobbamock's Homesite (where interpreters speak modern-day English), you can perhaps watch a canoe being built or visit the wetuash (houses). Hobbanock was a Pokanoket Indian and Plymouth Colony's interpreter and guide. Older children and adults will get more out of this museum than smaller children.

The Mayflower II is part of the museum complex although it is located on the Plymouth waterfront. As you can probably surmise from the ship's name, this is a re-creation of what the original Mayflower that brought the pilgrims to New England might have been like. You'll also find costumed interpreters on board more than willing to tell you how hard sailing over the ocean was in 1620. There are exhibits placed right outside the ship explaining why the Pilgrims left England, which native people they encountered on arrival, and navigation techniques. The kids can have fun playing games their 17th century counterparts played, such as bubbles.

Plymouth Rock
Plymouth Waterfront

A hop, skip and a jump from the Mayflower II, is that most-famous rock, Plymouth Rock. Supposedly, the pilgrims used the stone when stepping out of their ship. It's hard not to be disappointed when you see it; after all it's just a rock. Try to remember its symbolic meaning as the place where the pilgrims first landed.

Southwick's Zoo
2 Southwick Street
Mendon, MA 01756
508-883-9182, www.southwickszoo.com
Open: mid-April-October, 10am-5pm
Admission: Adults, $14.50; children 3-12, $10.50

Why should I drive an hour and pay an arm and a leg to go to a zoo, you ask? Well, the sheer size of this zoo and the numbers of animals it has makes it the largest zoo in New England. Prices are a little steep because it's privately owned. Like Davis Farmland, the Southwick's Zoo was once a real working farm.

Prepare to spend all day here because that's the only way you'll even see half of the animals on the 300-acre zoo. You'll probably get caught up attending presentations and shows offered throughout the day. The 35-acre deer forest is a great exhibit. You can buy feed, stroll through the forest and the deer will come eat right out of your hand! Southwick's Zoo is also more than just a showcase for animals. Earth Limited operates from the zoo, educating the public about environmentalism and animal ecology. A petting zoo, rides, and playground made completely out of recycled materials will certainly call to your kids.

World's End
250 Martins Lane
Hingham, MA
781-821-2977, www.thetrustees.org
Open 8am until sunset.
Admission: Adults, $4.50; under 12, free.

You might be surprised to see Frederick Law Olmsted's name popping up here, but yes, he did have a plan for this section of Hingham. In the 19th century John Brewer, who owned the land, wanted to parcel it in house plots and hired Olmsted to design the grounds. Luckily for us, only the good remains, as the development never happened. The Trustees for Preservation bought the land and set it aside for public use. Olmsted's paths and walkways remain and there are no houses to spoil the view. Hiking and walking are the main activities on the 200-plus-acre peninsula. Archaeologists think that the site was a seasonal campsite for Native Americans. We go there seasonally too. In warm weather, it's a great place to just kick back and have a picnic. This is no place for a stroller, though. Bring a kiddie backpack for the small ones.

The Trustees also have a variety of programs at World's End that should interest children. Say you have an early riser in the family. You might enjoy an informal bird walk on a Saturday morning at 7am ($4; kids under 12 free). Or maybe your kid has the makings of an animal tracker (just don't ask him to find his lost shoe). On snow days he or she can learn what animals are busy in the winter and what their tracks look like ($4.50; under 12, free). Call about the many other events scheduled throughout the year.

Seven: The Islands

Nantucket & Martha's Vineyard

Often mentioned in the same breath, Nantucket and Martha's Vineyard are two very different places, even when it comes down to their kid-friendliness. Though both islands can be visited as a day trip, it makes for a very long day, particularly for small children, so an overnight stay is in order. Two nights are best so you can have at least one leisurely day at the beach. The larger island inns are fine for children. I wouldn't recommend staying at a bed and breakfast except with older children. Generally, B&B guests are looking for peace and quiet. Also, antiques and kids aren't a good mix.

You can drive or take a bus to where the ferries wait to take you across to either island, at various spots on Cape Cod, or you can fly. There are pricey commuter flights available from Boston's Logan International Airport as well as Hyannis, though most people (including me) take a ferry. It's pretty much a straight shot down Route 3 to the various ferry points There are two ferry services available and both have overnight parking facilities. Call the Steamship Authority (508-477-8600; www.islandferry.com) or Hy-Line Cruises (800-492-8082; www.hy-linecruises.com). If you decide to take the bus, call Bonanza Bus Line (800-556-3815; www.bonazabus.com) for times and prices.

Going to Nantucket: The Steamship Authority runs car ferries from Hyannis that take two hours and fifteen minutes to Nantucket Town. No reservations are required for passengers and bicycles. If you are planning on taking a car however, you need to make reservations, in season, many months in advance. You can also just show up and play the odds at the standby queue, but this is not a sport for the faint of heart. The Hy-Line runs a high-speed passenger-only ferry from Hyannis that cuts the travel time down to an hour but is more costly than Steamship Authority. They also run a two-hour conventional passenger ferry. Reservations are strongly recommended, particularly in the summer season.

Going to the Vineyard: The Steamship Authority ferry ride is only 45 minutes from Woods Hole to Vineyard Haven. In the summer, several boats a day run to Oak Bluffs instead of

Vineyard Haven. If you have the choice, ride to Oak Bluffs. The Hy-Line runs only a conventional ferry from Hyannis to Vineyard Haven. The ride lasts an hour and thirty-five minutes.

Martha's Vineyard

Chamber of Commerce
Box 1698
Vineyard Haven, MA 02568
508-693-0085, www.mvy.com

Nobody is really quite sure where this large rural island got its name. The "Vineyard," as it is referred to by the initiated, can be easily seen in a day trip, but it only reveals its gentle charms when there is time to linger and explore. Though faced with the same conundrum of development versus preservation that confront all the last great places in the world, the Vineyard retains an unpolished, "just folks" rural character, which is a little bit deceiving. Spotting movie stars and other famous faces is a favorite tourist past time – many well-known people make their home here. The island is divided roughly into down-island and up-island.

Vineyard Haven, prudishly renamed so by Victorian sensibilities offended by the original moniker "Holmes Hole," is the main port of arrival for the ferries. Many island tour buses await day-trippers here in the summertime and are well worth the price if you need a quick guided overview of the island. There is also public transportation, rental car agencies and bike rental shops right by the dock. Paved bike trails link the three down-island towns and also provide access to off-road trails in the State Forest, a large preserve that surrounds the airport in the center of the island. Near the ferry landing a short stroll along the sand brings you to a small harbor beach and playground. There is a lifeguard on duty in the summer. If you decide to walk along the shore, please note that in Massachusetts property lines extend to the low tide line and some people have no tolerance for trespassers.

When it's time to eat, head to the **Black Dog Tavern** (Beach Street Extension, 508-693-9223). Though the thought of joining the hordes of people sporting the ubiquitous black lab silhouette T-shirts and sweatshirts may give you the willies, this Vineyard institution is quite good. The service is friendly, the waterfront location is beautiful, the ambiance is authentic and the menu is inventive, eclectic and kid friendly. Though the waits tend to be long, the kids can run on the beach, stroll on the pier and watch the ferries and boats come and go. The town is dry so BYOB. True story: One wintry day when we came to the island for the holiday festivals in December my daughter didn't want to come in from playing in the snow. I made her. Tears ensued, but moments later our server showed up at the table with a gigantic bowl of snow, forever winning my gratitude.

Oak Bluffs: This town has its roots in religious revivals of the mid-19th century, when a huge tent would be set up and a town of tents would house worshippers who came in increasing numbers attracted in equal measure by piety and pleasure. Eventually the tents were replaced by Victorian gingerbread cottages that still give the campgrounds (as they are still called) a decidedly Disney-esque feel, except, this is the real thing. The Victorian architecture is everywhere in the town and makes for a charming tour. The town is also traditionally an African-American vacation spot dating back to the turn of the century; is home to the famous Inkwell Beach; and has the lion's share of the sites on the Vineyard's African American Heritage Trail.

Victorian Houses in Oak Bluffs

Circuit Avenue (Oak Bluffs' main drag) and the harbor area are the closest that the Vineyard comes to the clamshack ambiance of mainland Cape Cod. Circuit Ave. is the best place to spot celebrities, so keep your eyes peeled for Carly Simon, Spike Lee, Dan Akroyd and other celebrities (not that your kids will know who they are).

The **Flying Horses carousel** anchors one of the busiest intersections of the island and is a must for all children. This is the oldest operating carousel in the nation: the beautiful, though sober, horses sport real horsehair manes. Going for the brass ring to the sounds of the calliope will enchant the children and bring the adults back to a real or imagined childhood. As the town peters out when walking down Circuit Avenue, there is a good playground down Massasoit Avenue toward Waban Park.

There are several spots to eat at. Try **Offshore Ale** (30 Kennebec Avenue; 508-693-2626). The sawdust on the floor almost screams kid-friendly and the barrel of roasted peanuts in their shells reinforces that thought. This microbrewery tavern offers a friendly atmosphere and a simple menu consisting of pub fare and pizzas. Linda Jean's Restaurant (34 Circuit Avenue; 508- 693-4093) is the quintessential diner, excellent for breakfast, and is what IHOP strives to be and fails. Fluffy pancakes smothered in fruit and other breakfast yummies.

Edgartown is the grande dame of the down-island towns that became rich in the 19th century (along with Nantucket) on whaling profits, and is still filled with the stately white, clapboarded federal-style mansions of the whaling captains. Definitely the tonier of the island towns, Main Street is filled with clothing and jewelry stores, restaurants and art galleries where Pissarros share exhibition space with local artists. The Harbor bustles in the summer season with sailboats of all sizes and the fourth of July parade and fireworks is a preserved piece of Rockwellian Americana

Right in Edgartown stands the **Edgartown light** that was turned into an understated and moving memorial to children taken from us before their time. I dare any parent to visit it and not at least feel the tears well up in their eyes. The walk to the light is beautiful and the right length, even for toddlers. A quiet harbor beach surrounds the light.

On the outskirts of town, just across from the cemetery, there is a small **firefighting museum** where children can play on a 1920s fire engine, including its hand-cranked, very loud, siren.

On a slow day the firefighters may come over and invite you to bring the kids in to look at the working fire station with its ladder trucks and other rescue equipment. It is quite a treat and always rewarding to kids.

From Edgartown you can also take the ironically named **"On Time" ferry** (it leaves as soon as it is full and, hence, is by definition always 'on time'). It goes to the island of **Chappaquidick**. "Chappy" has some of the most beautiful beaches and nature walks on the island. Our favorite for kids is the back harbor beach in the Wasque preserve, muddy flats that extend for miles with the water rarely reaching your knees. "Three-inch beach," as we have nicknamed it, is crowded only by horseshoe crabs, seagulls, terns and piping plovers, even in July and August. The adults can also walk over the dunes a few steps to access a beautiful Atlantic Ocean beach. Please note that there are no convenience stores at all in Chappy so make sure to bring along supplies, particularly water.

The **Newes from America Pub** (23 Kelly Street; 508-627-4397) is a long-time favorite spot for lunch. Excellent pub fare and a good kid's menu are served in a down-to-earth atmosphere. One great place to stay with kids is the Colonial Inn in Edgartown (800-627-4701; www.colonialinnmvy.com). This inn, built in 1912, is kid-friendly, with a library and games available for use. Some rooms have kitchenettes, so you can save on eating out. A complimentary breakfast is also offered and the views from the inn are spectacular. In season a room with two double beds is around $250. There are dozens of places to stay on the Vineyard, but booking early is imperative. Visit the Chamber of Commerce's webpage for listings.

Nantucket

Chamber of Commerce
48 Main Street
Nantucket, MA 02554
508-228-1700, www.nantucketchamber.org

Thirty miles out to sea from Hyannis, the "gray lady" is truly a land far away with its own unique beauty and a contrast from today's Cape Cod. Though it has recently been subjected to development pressure that is threatening to undermine its charm and character, the island is still filled with beautifully understated homes, open natural spaces and unspoiled beaches. Nantucket is quite pricey, particularly as compared to Martha's Vineyard; it costs more to get there, it's more expensive to stay, more expensive to eat and is a very exclusive and upper-crust, old money destination where hundred-foot yachts are a common sight in summer.

If you did not bring a car, you will need a bike to use on the many miles of paved bike trails on the island. Renting a car here is an expensive proposition and the island is small enough and destinations are close enough that you will have no problem without a car, even with kids in bike seats or towing trailers. There are several bike rental places in Nantucket town, however I recommend **Young's Bicycle** at Steamboat Wharf, 617-228-1151.

The chief entertainment on the island is what you create yourself. Lazy days on the beach is as exciting as it gets. If your kids or you want a lot of excitement, you'd be better off on Martha's Vineyard.

In **Nantucket Town** federal style homes, elegant understated restaurants, charming shops and art galleries on cobblestone streets invite window shopping and leisurely strolls – not something you will be doing if you have toddlers in tow (too bad). However, there is a harbor beach appropriately named **"Children's Beach,"** an easy walk from town. It's ideal for small children and has a park with a new playground, game tables, and a bandstand. One the beach, there's a lifeguard, restrooms, showers, restaurant and take-out food service, and picnic tables. Restaurant, playground, and rest room are all wheelchair-accessible. Other beaches appropriate for children include Dionis and Jetties beaches, both easily accessible by bike trail.

The **Nantucket Maria Mitchell Association** (4 Vestal Street; 508-228-9198; www.mmo.org) runs a small aquarium, an observatory, a natural science museum and operates weeklong camps and day activities in season for children of all ages.
Food just tastes better in Nantucket and there is a definite island style.

The **Brotherhood of Thieves** (23 Broad Street). Burgers, specialty sandwiches and soups, wonderful, friendly atmosphere, music some nights. Careful though - they don't take credit cards.
Cap'n Tobey's Chowder House (Straight Wharf; 508-228-0836). A Nantucket institution, chowder, fresh seafood and an extensive children's menu
Brant Point Grill at the White Elephant (50 Easton St.; 800-475-2637; www.whiteelephanthotel.com). For a wonderful al fresco lunch, you can't beat the terrace at the White Elephant, where you can watch the sailboats go by in the harbor. Lots of room for the kids to roam. This is also one of the best places to stay with kids on the island. For more accommodations options call the Chamber of Commerce.

Fun at the beach!

Eight: Appendix

Hints for Bargain Hunters

Try to visit tourist-heavy sites during the week. There is no real non-tourist season in Boston and weekends find them, and natives, out in droves no matter what time of year it is, but weekdays are a bit less crowded.

Go during lunchtime if you can. Decide if you can eat early, or late, and bring snacks and water. Not everyone else will have thought of this, so while they are waiting in long concession lines, you'll have a little more room to breathe. And you'll save money while you're at it. Food is never cheap at a museum.

Do your homework. Read the next section on freebies and find out how to get bargains. No one is going to volunteer that there are often two-for-one tickets or specials deals available. You have to ask. It's a bummer to find out that if you had just come the day before or waited a couple of hours, your visit could have been free or discounted.

It's not cheap to travel, especially in Boston. If you can do a little extra legwork and schedule carefully there are all sorts of deals to be had. Bostonians are notoriously frugal, so you'll have the added bonus of doing as the natives do.

Here are a few pointers, but these may change at any time. If you can, call or visit the website of every place you think you might visit to see what their latest deals are. At the very least, call the Boston Tourist Board to get their tourist information. You can also order a useful guide from the tourist board, called "Kids Love Boston" geared for children. It has fun facts and games inside. (Call 888-SEE-BOSTON.)

These following attractions have free or discounted entry fees on certain days.

Museum of Fine Arts: Free admission on Wednesday after 4pm (contribution voluntary); On Thursdays and Fridays after 5pm, get $2 off tickets. All tickets are good for two days.
Harvard Museums: Free admission on Sunday, 9am-noon; Wednesday from 3-5pm.
Children's Museum: Fridays, $1 admission after 5pm.
Franklin Park Zoo: Free admission until noon, first Saturday of the month.

More Discounts & Deals
Call or visit to buy advance or discount tickets to all sorts of sights in the city at the following places.

BosTix
617-482-BTIX
BosTix booths: Copley Square & Faneuil Hall Marketplace
www.boston.com/artsboston
Open: Copley kiosk hours are Mon.-Sat., 10am-6 pm; Sunday, 11am-4pm; closed Patriot's Day, Thanksgiving, Christmas. Faneuil Hall kiosk hours are similar except it is closed on Mondays.

If you can be flexible, this is a great way to save money. BosTix sells half-price, day-of-the-show tickets to all sorts of arts events around town. They also sell full-price advance tickets and serve as a Ticketmaster outlet. They accept cash only.

Boston CityPass
Call 707-256-0490
www.citypass.com
Cost: Adult, $36.75, children 3-17, $25.50

This pass is good for the following six attractions in the city: Museum of Science, Museum of Fine Arts, Boston, New England Aquarium, John F. Kennedy Library and Museum, Skywalk Observatory and the Harvard Museum of Natural History. It's a great idea for those on a serious sightseeing trip. You can buy the pass at any of the attractions. It's good for nine days, starting from the day you buy it. You not only save 50% off ticket prices, but once you buy the pass, you can skip the ticket lines at the rest of the sites you visit.

MBTA Visitor's Passport
You can buy an unlimited travel pass for one day ($7.50); three days, ($18); or seven days ($35). This pass is good for train and bus service. Call the MBTA at 617-222-3200 for more info or to order your passes in advance, or you can visit their visit their website at www.mbta.com.

Bathroom Breaks
It's always a good idea to scout out bathrooms when traveling around. I try to find the nearest bookstore and, fortunately, Boston is filled with bookstores. Many of them even have bathrooms right in the children's section complete with diaper-changing stations. Libraries are usually my next choice. All towns have one and they can't tell you no. Believe it or not, there's a whole section dedicated to public restrooms, with a users rating scale, at www.boston-online.com/restrooms. Hotels seem to top the list, followed by malls and restaurants.

Kim Foley MacKinnon

Calendar of Events

January
Annual New Year's Day swim: Join or watch the L Street Swimming Club Brownies in their traditional dip in South Boston. 617-635-5104.
Japanese New Year: Celebrate at the Children's Museum. Arts & crafts, demonstrations, music and more. 617-451-0726.

February
Chinese New Year: 617-635-3485

March
New England Spring Flower Show: Remind yourself spring is coming at the annual flower show at the Bayside Exposition Center. 617-536-9280.
St. Patrick's Day Parade/Evacuation Day (Massachusetts holiday): 617-536-4100.

April
Patriot's Day/Boston Marathon:
The oldest marathon in the US. Finish line in Copley Square. 617-236-1652; www.bostonmarathon.com. Patriot's Day parade leaves from City Hall at 9:30am followed by reenactment of Paul Revere's ride. 617-635-4447.
Swan Boats Return to Public Garden

May
Lilac Sunday: View 250 different blooms at Arnold Arboretum. 617-524-1718.

Make Way for Ducklings Parade: (Mother's Day) Register at noon at Boston Common to march like a duck. 617-426-1885.
Kite Festival: Make, fly or just watch at Franklin Park. 617-635-4505.

June
Art in the Park Festival (DeCordova Museum): Activities for children; music; entertainment. 781-259-8355.
Bunker Hill Day (Boston holiday): Re-enactments; parade. 617-242-5628.
Concerts at the Hatch Shell: Come hear music or see a performance. 617-727-5251.
Dragon Boat Festival: Beautifully decorated boats race on the Charles. 617-426-6500, ext. 778, www.bostondragonboat.org
Scooper Bowl: Delicious ice cream fundraiser. 800-52JIMMY.
Free Friday Flicks at the Hatch Shell. 617-727-5114, ext.530; www.state.ma.us/mdc.

July
Boston Pops Fourth of July Concert: At the Hatchshell. 617-266-1492.
Chowderfest: Gorge on chowder at this July 4th tradition at City Hall Plaza.
617-227-1528; www.bostonharborfest.com/chowderfest/.
Harborfest: Boston celebrates the waterfront with events through the week. 617-227-1528. www.bostonharborfest.com
North End Italian Festivals: Celebrating saints with feasts and parades. 617-536-4100.

August
August Moon Festival: Chinatown festival. Parade, music and food. 617-542-2574.

North End Italian Feasts: Celebrate the saints all summer. 617-635-3911.

September
The Big E: The Eastern States Exposition in Springfield, MA, has agricultural events, amusement rides, music, parades and more. 800-334-BIGE; www.thebige.com.

October
Head of the Charles Regatta: Racing on the Charles River. 617-864-8415; www.hocr.org.
Lantern Festival: Dusk festival at Jamaica Pond.

November
Veteran's Day Parade: The 1pm parade kicks off in the Back Bay. 617-635-3911.
Boston Ballet's Nutcracker: The annual favorite at the Wang Center. 800-447-7400; www.bostonballet.org.
Enchanted Village: Visit an animated re-creation of a turn-of-the-century village on a snowy Christmas Eve at City Hall Plaza. 617-635-3689.
Teddy Bear Tea: Do good and have fun at the annual Teddy Bear Tea at the Omni Parker House, a charity event to benefit needy children. 978-356-2602. www.teddybeardrive.org.
Holiday Lighting Ceremony: Kick off the season at Faneuil Hall's Lighting Ceremony. Performances and food all day. 617-523-1300. www.faneuilhallmarketplace.com.
Boston Common Frog Pond: The pond opens up for ice-skating. 617-635-2120.

December

Winter Wonderland Train Display: Check out the 400 feet of track laid out at South Station. Little villages, bridges and tunnels make a charming scene.

Tree Lightings: The two biggies are the Prudential Holiday Tree Lighting and the Boston Common Holiday Lighting the first weekend of this month. www.bostonusa.com.

Christmas Revels: Winter Solstice celebration at Harvard's Sanders Theatre. Every year features a different theme. 617-469-2222.

First Night: New Year's Eve celebration for everyone, with more than 250 events throughout the city. Buy a button to gain admission to all the festivities in dozens of venues. 617-542-1399; www.firstnight.org.

Helpful Numbers & Websites

Greater Boston Convention & Visitors Bureau
2 Copley Place, Suite 105
Boston, Ma 02116
617-536-4100; 888-SEE-BOSTON
www.bostonusa.com
One-stop shopping here. Information on everything Boston. Very helpful site helps you plan your trip with tips, prices, and more. Links to other websites make it easy to figure out what you want to do. Go to the Family Friendly Values section for special deals.

Boston and Massachusetts websites
www.cityofboston.com/calendar/calendar.asp

A great website to find out what's going on when you are visiting. Recurring and one-day events are listed. You can search by neighborhood, date, or event.

Boston-Online
www.boston-online.com
Very useful site with link to all sorts of Boston stuff, including where to find public bathrooms and Boston etiquette. It's a humorous but accurate site that doesn't take itself seriously. It offers little-known facts about Beantown.

Cambridge Office for Tourism
4 Brattle Street, Suite 208
Cambridge, MA 02138
617-441-2884; 800-862-5678; www.cambridge-usa.org

Destination Plymouth
225 Water Street, Suite 202
Plymouth, MA 02360
508-747-7533; 800-USA-1620; www.visit-plymouth.com

Destination Salem
59 Wharf Street, Suite C-2
Salem, MA 01970
978-744-3663; 877-SALEMMA
www.salem.org

GoCityKids
www.gocitykids.com
This fabulous website has the lowdown on everything to do around Boston with children complete with a daily calendar. Check it out for the days you are visiting to see what's going on. You can sign up for a newsletter updating you on events.

Greater Merrimack Valley Convention & Visitors Bureau
9 Central St., Suite 201
Lowell, MA 01852
800-433-3332; 978-459-6150
www.lexington-concord.org
Covers Lexington, Concord and Lowell.

Mass Vacations
www.massvacations.com
Make reservations for hotels, B & Bs and inns.

MBTA
617-722-3200; www.mbta.com

Nantucket Island Chamber of Commerce
48 Main Street
Nantucket, MA 02554
508-228-0659; www.nantucketchamber.org

Martha's Vineyard Chamber of Commerce
Box 1698
Vineyard Haven, MA 02568
508-693-0085; www.mvy.com

Author's Last Word

A version of the following essay appeared in The Boston Globe *in 2003. It explains a bit about what I love about Boston and why I chose to live here and raise a family.*

Boston is not the friendliest of cities to raise a child in. Don't get me wrong. I love Boston. I've even written a guidebook about the many charms of the city for families. But, for every upside, there is a downside.

Sure, there are a lot of great destinations, but how will you get there? Transportation, a hassle for all Bostonians, is compounded when you have children. Do you take your kid, or kids, in the car and hope against hope for a parking space, or do forgo the car and take public transportation? If you drive and can't find a space, you have to pony up big bucks for a garage. If you are visiting one of our many fine institutions, such as the Children's Museum, New England Aquarium or Museum of Science, all popular family magnets, garages are necessary and exorbitant. Of course, this is all irrelevant if you get lost on Boston's unmarked, one-way streets. But if you lose your way in the maze that is the Big Dig, and go home in disgust, you can always tell your kids that you were on a field trip to the world's biggest construction site.

Buses and trains can be adventures in themselves for little kids, but should you opt for public transportation, don't take a stroller. Many MBTA subway stops have inconvenient, nonexistent, or smelly elevators. Bus drivers seem to have an intense dislike of parents hauling strollers and manage to drive by without seeing you. Once aboard a packed train or bus, don't think anyone will give up a seat for your kid either. And if you have a kiddie backpack, plan on standing. They are impossible to get off if you are alone and good luck getting assistance from chilly New Englanders just minding their own business.

If you are determined to bring a stroller, you will regret it, especially if you are sightseeing. Cobblestone streets, historic buildings with no elevators, and no place to store them once you get there, are the first things that come to mind.

While you are wandering around Boston's streets, try explaining to your kid why all the grown-ups cross against the light despite the "Don't Walk" signs flashing. Even when the "Walk" sign is on, it's a dangerous proposition to make it to the other side of the road. We always run.

Once you have managed to get to the Children's Museum via the awful pedestrian bridge, you have to explain why your homemade lunch beats out a Happy Meal from McDonald's, which is connected to the museum. How can anyone in their right mind think that it is appropriate to have a fast food restaurant here? It's outrageous that a place where children are encouraged to explore and think and learn should be nestled with one of the reasons children are so overweight in this country. On top of that, there is nowhere except the cold hard floor to sit on should you pack a lunch and it's too cold to go outside.

Even if you firmly believe the suburbs aren't for you, you still have to venture there to buy baby supplies, furniture and toys. Sure, there is FAO Schwartz on Boylston Street, but this not an inexpensive store. You have to drive to those big box stores where you can get cribs, car seats and children's furniture. They just don't carry jumbo boxes of diapers at CVS.

Getting around for family excursions is one thing, but it can get even more complicated to get your kids back and forth to school. With the Boston Public School lottery system, it is feasible your child might be across town attending classes.

Figuring out the system is more difficult than applying to college. This is one of the top reasons people flee the city for the suburbs.

However, when I start to complain about the traffic, the schools and the inconvenience, I think about the suburbanites who go from their smoothly paved driveways to the mall in their DVD-equipped minivans and stop at the McDonald's drive-through. I think about their 45-minute commutes to work, or to anywhere else. It may be convenient, but it's way too quiet. No thanks. I'll stay where I am.

Like the song says, "Boston, you're my home."

Index

147

Kim Foley MacKinnon

Printed in the United States
18934LVS00001B/259-348

9 781591 135067